Indians of the
Great Basin

BIBLIOGRAPHICAL SERIES
*The Newberry Library Center
for the History of the American Indian*

General Editor
Francis Jennings

Assistant Editor
William R. Swagerty

The Center is Supported by Grants from

The National Endowment for the Humanities
The Ford Foundation
The W. Clement and Jessie V. Stone Foundation
The Woods Charitable Fund, Inc.
Mr. Gaylord Donnelley
The Andrew W. Mellon Foundation
The Robert R. McCormick Charitable Trust
The John D. and Catherine T. McArthur Foundation

Indians of the Great Basin

A Critical Bibliography

OMER C. STEWART

Published for the Newberry Library

Indiana University Press

Bloomington

Manufactured in the United States of America

Library of Congress Cataloging in Publication Data

Stewart, Omer Call, 1908–
    Indians of the Great Basin.

    (Bibliographical series / The Newberry Library Center for the History of the American Indian)
    Includes index.
    1. Indians of North America — Great Basin — Bibliography. I. Title. II. Series: Bibliographical series (Newberry Library. Center for the History of the American Indian)
Z1209.2.U52G736 [E78.G67]   016.979'00497   81–48084
ISBN 0–253–32979–5 (pbk.)   AACR2
1 2 3 4 5 86 85 84 83 82

CONTENTS

PREFACE

The Indians of the Great Basin are an admirable example of human adaptiveness to harsh circumstances. Living within the sagebrush deserts and numerous mountain ranges situated between the Sierra Nevada and Cascade mountains of California and Oregon in the west and the Rocky Mountains of Colorado and Wyoming in the east, Numic-speaking peoples and their predecessors are historically connected with the technological complex of hunting and gathering peoples. They did not have the advantages afforded by agriculture and plentiful supplies of fresh water, and were therefore dependent almost exclusively upon the gathering of wild plants and the hunting of animals.

For purposes of this essay the Great Basin will be considered that territory occupied by the Numic speakers in historic times. The tribes in question are the Shoshonis, Northern Paiutes, Bannocks, Utes, Southern Paiutes, plus the Washoes, a small non-Numic people who lived in extreme western Nevada. The latter lived in the vicinity of modern Reno and Carson City and spent their summers around Lake Tahoe.

Because their lifestyle and material culture were not as spectacular as other tribes on their borders to European and American observers, Indians of the Great Basin have not attracted as many scholarly or popular publications as their neighbors. Nevertheless, the literature on the Basin is vast. Within the past twenty years we have learned much about the prehistory of the region and, although much remains to be written, great progress has been made in understanding the origins, lifestyles and early history of these tribes.

Great Basin as presented here is designated "Basin" in volume 3 of the fourth edition of Murdock and O'Leary's *Ethnographic Bibliography of North America* [213]. Their map is very similar to Map 1 of this volume, although ten groups are named occupying the area assigned to six in this study. The wide availability of Murdock and O'Leary renders it an essential starting point for research on the literature of peoples of the region. However, those two authors have appropriately noted that "the bibliography compiled by Catherine S. Fowler [54] is probably the most complete bibliography for any area in North America ...". Over one thousand titles are listed by Fowler and the serious scholar will want to consult this important bibliographic tool.

The following essay presents and evaluates the major publications in Great Basin archaeology, ethnohistory and ethnography. A section on historical sources is included, but this is by no means an exhaustive survey.

RECOMMENDED WORKS

For the Beginner

[10]   Paul Bailey, *Walkara, Hawk of the Mountains.*

[11]   Paul Bailey, *Wovoka, The Indian Messiah.*

[46]   James F. Downs, *The Two Worlds of the Washo.*

[83]   Nellie Shaw Harnar, *Indians of Coo-yu-ee Pah (Pyramid Lake).*

[115]   Inter-Tribal Council of Nevada, *NEWE: A Western Shoshone History.*

[116]   ———. *NUMA: A Northern Paiute History.*

[117]   ———. *NUWUVI: A Southern Paiute History.*

[118]   ———. *WA SHE SHU: A Washo Tribal History.*

[125]   James Jefferson, Robert W. Delaney, and Gregory C. Thompson, *The Southern Utes: A Tribal History.*

[328]   Uintah-Ouray Ute Tribe, *A Brief History of the Ute People.*

[342]   Walker River Paiute Tribe, *Walker River Paiute: A Tribal History.*

[354]   E. N. Wilson, *The White Indian Boy.*

For a Basic Library Collection

[14]   Stephen F. Bedwell, *Fort Rock Basin: Prehistory and Environment.*

[19]   Herbert E. Bolton, *Pageant in The Wilderness.*

[28]   Gloria G. Cline, *Exploring the Great Basin.*

[39]   Warren L. d'Azevedo, ed., *The Washo Indians.*

[40]   Warren L. d'Azevedo, et al., *The Current Status of Anthropological Research in the Great Basin.*

[47]   Cora Du Bois, *The 1870 Ghost Dance.*

[60]   Don D. Fowler and Catherine S. Fowler, eds., *Anthropology of the Numa.*

[87]   C. V. Haynes, Jr., "The Earliest Americans."

[89]   Grace R. Hebard, *Washakie.*

[102] Sarah Winnemuca Hopkins, *Life Among the Piutes.*

[126] Jesse D. Jennings, *Danger Cave.*

[128] Jesse D. Jennings, *Prehistory of North America.*

[134] Joseph G. Jorgensen, *The Sun Dance Religion.*

[150] Carobeth Laird, *The Chemehuevi.*

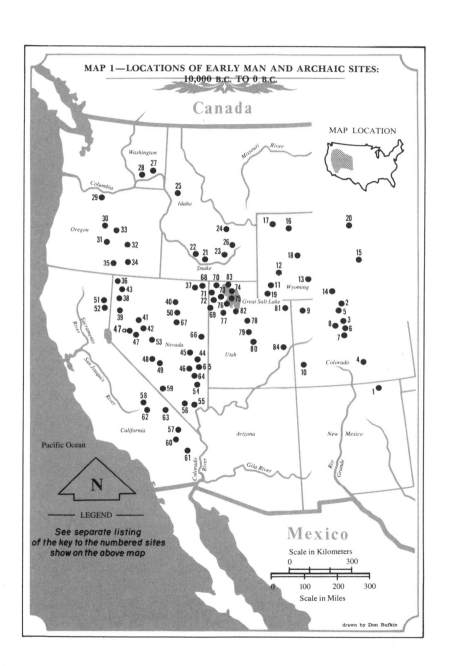

MAP 1—LOCATIONS OF EARLY MAN AND ARCHAIC SITES: 10,000 B.C. TO 0 B.C.

drawn by Don Bufkin

Key to map locations

MAP 1—LOCATIONS OF EARLY MAN AND ARCHAIC SITES: 10,000 B.C. to 0 B.C.

New Mexico
1—Folsom

Colorado
2—Lindenmeir
3—Dent
4—Linger and Zapata
5—Gordon Creek and Johnson
6—Lamb Spring
7—Kassler
8—LoDaiska
9—Dinosaur/Hell's Midden
10—Tabegauche

Wyoming
11—Black's Fork
12—Finley/Eden
13—U.P.
14—Jimmy Allen
15—Hell's Gap
16—Horner/Cody
17—Mummy Cave
18—Birdshead Cave
19—Pine Spring
20—McKean

Idaho and S.E. Washington
21—Wilson Butte Cave
22—Simon Cave
23—American Falls/Haskett
24—Birch Creek/Jaguar Cave
25—Weis Rockshelter
26—Wasden/Owl Cave
27—Marmes Rockshelter
28—Lind Coulee

Oregon
29—Five Mile Rapids
30—Fort Rock
31—Paisley
32—Roaring Springs
33—Cougar Mountain
34—Catlow
35—Guano

Nevada and California
36—Massacre Lake/High Rock
37—Deer Creek Cave
38—Black Rock Desert
39—Winnemucca Lake Caves

40—Carlin
41—Lovelock/Humboldt
42—Leonard Rock Shelter
43—Smokey Creek
44—Caliente
45—Dry Lakes
46—Groom Dry Lake
47—Hidden Cave/Falon
47a—Sadmat
48—Tonapah
49—Mud Lake
50—South Fork Rock Shelter
51—Karlo
52—Tommy Tucker Cave
53—Wagon Jack Shelter
54—Etna Cave
55—Gypsum Cave
56—Tule Spring
57—Lake Mohave
58—Rose Spring
59—Beatty
60—Newberry Cave
61—Pinto Basin
62—Stahl

63—Death Valley
64—Conaway Shelter
65—O'Malley Shelter
66—Amy's Shelter/Smith Creek Cave
67—Neward Cave
68—No Name Valley

Utah
69—Danger Cave
70—Beatty Spring
71—Swallow Shelter
72—Remnant Cave
73—Hogup Cave
74—Promontory Caves
75—Fremont Island
76—Stansbury Caves
77—Dugway
78—Spotten Cave
79—Joe's Valley
80—Clyde's Cavern
81—Deluge Shelter
82—Black Rock and Deadman Caves
83—Curlew Valley
84—Moab

see map on previous page

BIBLIOGRAPHICAL ESSAY

Prehistory

Evidences of Paleo-Indian occupation of the Americas have been found in numerous sites dated at or about 10,000 B.P. (before present). It was in 1926 that J. D. Figgins, a paleontologist from the Denver Museum of Natural History, found the first indisputable evidence that a large, now-extinct bison was killed by man. The fossil bones were in a geological deposit about 10,000 years old and among the bones was a well shaped stone projectile point, so peculiar that it was named for the site—Folsom. Whenever found in natural surroundings these projectile points have indicated early man occupation as discussed in Hannah Marie Wormington's *Ancient Man in North America* [359].

Early man sites have been found most frequently east of the Rocky Mountains, just over the ridges from the territory of Great Basin Indians, as discussed by George C. Frison [65] and Joe Ben Wheat [347]. Some have also been found in the Great Basin, and even west of the Sierra Nevada Mountains in California as outlined in M. R. Harrington's, *An Ancient Site at Borax Lake, California* [84]. The Folsom points and other distinctive types of chipped stone implements if found only at a kill site or on the surface, do not tell much about the way of life of early man. Fortunately occupation sites and some ancient living floors have been discovered. The first site discovered that shows how Folsom families lived 10,000 years ago was near Fort Collins, Colorado, and was called the Lindenmeir Site. Edwin N. Wilmsen's *Lindenmeir* [353] is a final report of investigations from 1934 to 1974. Students seeking a broad overview of the site's importance should see Wilmsen's *Lindenmeier: A Pleistocene Hunting Society* [352] and the most recent edition of Wormington's *Ancient Man in North America* [359].

Also just beyond the eastern edge of the Great Basin in Wyoming ancient man sites have been found in Hell Gap Valley. The reports on these sites were made by C. Irwin-Williams, H. Irwin and G. Agogino in 1973 [123]. Having excavated the Mammoth kill at Hell Gap, which the excavators asserted was the oldest evidence of man in the New World, they were fortunate to be nearby when railroad construction on the lowest pass in the Rocky Mountains exposed another Mammoth site. It was named the U.P. Site and dated 9,300 B.C. A summary of the importance of the findings was published as "Ice Age Man versus Mammoth in Wyoming" [122]. Irwin compared his own data with that of other Great Basin early man sites in his doctoral dissertation [120] and in a subsequent article entitled "Developments in Early Man Studies in Western North America" [121]. Great Basin early man sites used for comparison by Irwin were the U.P. Site in Wyoming; Wilson Butte Cave, American Falls and Simon, Idaho; and, Tule Springs, Nevada.

The evidence of ancient man in Idaho has been published in *Tebiwa* and *Occasional Papers,* publications started in 1958 at Idaho State University Museum. Gruhn [75] excavated and reported Wilson Butte Cave, an important site dated at 8,000 B.C. This cave contained remains of the horse *Equis* and the camel *Camelops* with tools on the lowest level, yet modern Shoshonean pottery was found near the surface. Another deep cave which was occupied for a great length of time, and nearly contemporaneous with Wilson Butte Cave, was Fort Rock Cave in central Oregon excavated by Stephen F. Bedwell [14].

In Utah a fluted point, usually called Folsom, and a type of implement for ancient big game hunters on the Plains 10,000 years ago was reported found in south central Utah by J. H. Gunnerson [76]. Such a find could add only a few centuries to the date of the lowest levels of all such caves occupied for millenia. Danger Cave, reported by Jesse D. Jennings [126] and Hogup Cave by Melvin C. Aikens [3] are exemplary of this long occupancy by ancient hunters.

The Tule Springs Site is a good point of departure for review of Nevada prehistory. The site first gained fame because it was interpreted as one of the earliest sites occupied by man in the New World and was carbon-14 dated at 21,800 B.C. [85]. Extensive interdisciplinary reinvestigation of the Tule Springs Site was initiated in 1962 under the direction of Richard Shutler. His original findings were published as *Lost City: Pueblo Grande de Nevada* [263]. An update appeared as "Archaeology of Tule Springs" [264]. Geologist C. Vance Haynes, paleontologist John E. Mawley, palynologist Peter J. Mehringer, Jr., beographers W. Glen Bradley and James E. Deacon, and a host of archaeologists and other specialists assisted in one of the most massive scientific excavations known. Seven thousand feet of bulldozer trenching, averaging approximately fifteen feet in depth, provided the walls for careful mapping and sample collecting. Based upon geological evidence, early man may have been at Tule Springs 13,000 years ago, and was definitely there 10,000 years ago (8,000 B.C.). Only eleven artifacts were recovered from 700,000 tons of earth that was moved, indicating the often-frustrating experiences of archaeologists seeking early man data.

On the basis of the amount of earth removed and screened, a similar experience occurred at the Calico Mountain Site, located on the periphery of the Great Basin in present-day California. There, L. S. B. Leakey, famed for discoveries of early hominids in Olduvai Gorge, Tanzania, came to Southern California to try his luck at finding evidence of human occupation more ancient than most scholars believed likely. He supported Simpson and Clements in the belief that Calico Mountain artifacts were at least 50,000 years old and published his preliminary findings with them in 1968 [160]. Geologist Haynes speaks for many American archaeologists who reject the ancient stones from Calico as artifacts in his article, "The Calico Site: Artifacts or Geofacts?" [88].

Less controversial than Calico are other Mohave Desert cultures. San Dieguito is the name assigned to a prehistoric culture first found in the Mohave, but now recognized as having developed on the southern coast of California and further south in the deserts of Baja California. From 1929 to 1960, Malcolm J. Rogers wrote several reports of that culture. Rogers summarized these papers in the book, *Ancient Hunters of the Far West,* edited by Richard F. Pourade [249]. This well-illustrated anthology contains articles by H. M. Wormington, E. L. Davis and C. Brott as well as that by Rogers. The first map in the book is especially important for understanding the range of the San Dieguito Culture which extended from the mouth of the Colorado River north through the Mohave Desert and Death Valley along the eastern base of the Sierra Nevada Mountains into Oregon. This culture period is estimated to have been present in the Great Basin by 8,000 B.C.

The *Anthropological Papers of the Nevada State Museum* have earned a place of special importance because of the reports on early man sites. Starting with No. 13, *Pleistocene Studies in Southern Nevada,* edited by Wormington and Ellis [360], this series has contained a number of important early man discussions that should be consulted by the serious scholar. In 1969, the Nevada State Museum published an interesting technical paper regarding flintknapping by D. R. Tuohy. Tuohy [320] analyzed one hundred and forty-seven projectile points from four sites in western Nevada and concluded that the Lake Mohave points, datable at 8,000 B.C., should be classified as a co-tradition extending from Hell's Gap, Wyoming, to American Falls, Idaho; and on to Cougar Mountain, Oregon; and then south through Nevada to Mohave Desert, California—thus covering the extended Great Basin as defined for this essay. A companion article by Emma Lou Davis and Richard Shutler, Jr. [37], with an appendix by Donald R. Tuohy is also of note. Davis and Shutler report on twenty-eight fluted points from the Great Basin area of California. A map included in the paper shows seven eastern California sites and thirteen Nevada sites well distributed over the state. Tuohy adds the information that fifty-four additional fluted points have been recovered from extinct Lake Tonapah and Mud Lake. Tuohy believes these and the points illustrated by Davis and Shutler are Clovis points, contemporaneous to Folsom, and considers them evidence of extension across the Great Basin of the Clovis or Folsom culture of the western high Plains.

The name of L. L. Loud will always be important in Great Basin anthropology because of the relatively early date and continued importance of Lovelock Cave to Nevada prehistory, even though Loud published nothing else. Unfortunately, in 1911, Lovelock Cave was first dug into in order to remove two hundred and fifty tons of bat guano for fertilizer. The thousands of objects recovered in the process were scattered. The work of Loud and Harrington [168] in 1924 and others who have revisited the cave in order to place the material in context see it as of great importance. Basketry, nets, rabbit-skin blankets and duck-skin decoys are a few of the things which tied prehistoric cave dwellers to the modern Northern Paiute Indians of the area.

The Lovelock Cave report was the beginning of a long list of monographs and articles published by the University of California at Berkeley on the anthropology of Nevada. The archaeological work started by Loud in 1911 was carried on by Robert F. Heizer from 1940 to 1979. Heizer's first important excavation at Humboldt Cave in Nevada was accomplished in the summer of 1936. The results of this pioneering research were published with Alex D. Krieger in 1956 [93]. G. L. Grosscup produced a comparative summary, *The Culture History of Lovelock Cave, Nevada* [74] in 1960, and defined a Lovelock Culture area which includes seventeen sites in western Nevada and eastern California.

The establishment of the California Archaeological Survey in 1948, with Robert F. Heizer as director, marked the beginning of an accelerated rate of research and publication on the archaeology of the southwestern section of the Great Basin. Ten years after the establishment of the Survey, Heizer published an overview of *Current Views on Great Basin Archaeology* [91]. By 1968 seventy-four volumes had been published by the Survey and twenty-two of those volumes included some material on the Great Basin.

The Archaeology of the Karlo Site (Las-7), California, by Francis A. Riddell [247] followed the pattern of production set by Heizer and Krieger [93] and made a careful comparison of material recovered from the large open site on the extreme western edge of the central Great Basin, with artifacts recovered elsewhere, especially Danger Cave—five hundred miles to the east. Karlo projectile points are remarkably similar to those of Danger Cave for the period of time the two sites were both occupied. Riddell places 2,000 B.C. as the beginning of Karlo occupation, equal to the upper one-third of Danger Cave, about the time of Lovelock Cave occupation. Although similar enough in artifacts to be placed in the Lovelock Culture tradition, a number of traits tied Karlo to central California. Most remarkable were the thirteen skulls recovered which had closer affinity with California than with known Great Basin skeletal material.

Thomas R. Hester's *Chronological Ordering of Great Basin Prehistory* [96] is an important revision of his doctoral dissertation completed at California in 1972. Although he takes a restrictive physiographic view of the Great Basin, except for the inclusion of the Mohave Desert in southeastern California, Hester's report required thirty pages to list the references cited in the 167 pages of text, an indication of the burgeoning literature on the region in recent decades. Utilizing an ecological interpretation model, Hester reviewed data from geology, botany, and related fields, as well as from archaeology in reaching his conclusions. He subdivided Great Basin prehistory into four useful chronological periods: Period I (=10,000 to 5,000 B.C.); Period II (5,000 to 2,000 B.C.); Period III (2,000 B.C. to 0 A.D.); Period IV (1 A.D. to Present).

Great Basin prehistory shares some features with the Basketmaker and Pueblo cultures of the Southwest. The areas of similarity include decorated pottery, agriculture, and stone or clay brick houses. In Utah this culture is called Fremont. In Nevada it had its most complete manifestation along the lower Virgin River and its main Nevada tributary, the Muddy River. At one time the Muddy flowed passed Moapa, Overton and St. Thomas, Nevada; however, St. Thomas was flooded by the waters of Lake Mead, created by Boulder Dam in the 1930's. Archaeological reports of surveys of Puebloid Culture of extreme southern Nevada date back to M. S. Duffield's report of 1904 [48]. It was not until Richard Shutler, Jr. published *Lost City: Pueblo Grande de Nevada,* [263] that there was a comprehensive account of the prehistoric Pueblo culture of Nevada. Shutler made surveys of the area, but his doctoral thesis and book were based on notes, maps and photographs of M. R. Harrington, who completed the salvage archaeology from 1924 through 1938, just before the sites were flooded. The Museum of the American Indian of New York City, the National Park Service, the Southwest Museum and the Nevada State Museum were the caretakers of the notes and photographs utilized by Shutler for his monograph which contains useful maps, charts and photographs as well as a short text.

Archaeology has fascinated people of Utah. This is partly the result of the interest in history and prehistoric civilizations of Joseph Smith, founder of the

Church of Jesus Christ of Latter-Day Saints. At one time Mormons hoped to find evidence to support their belief that the American Indians were descendants of Hebrews migrating to the New World from Palestine between 2,200 B.C. and 588 B.C. Mormon interest was translated into action in 1900 when the president of Brigham Young University organized and led a twenty-man expedition to excavate sites in Mexico and South America. The rewards were so meager that the Mormon authorities gave no further active support to archaeology until 1941 when Brigham Young University organized a Department of Archaeology chaired by M. W. Jakeman. Many reports have since been published by this fine university.

Julian H. Steward, famous for his writings regarding the ethnology of the Great Basin, produced seven important publications from 1928 to 1941 regarding its prehistory. Although his major archaeological monographs were published by the Smithsonian Institution [281] [284]. Steward's research on Utah prehistory was published also by the University of Utah [277], the Museum of Northern Arizona [279], and the University of New Mexico [280]. The excavation of Promontary Cave [281], during which Shoshoni pottery and unusual moccasins were recovered, has required the greatest amount of attention by other archaeologists, whether for comparative purposes or for theory construction.

A new era of archaeology in Utah started with the appointment of Jesse D. Jennings to the faculty at the

University of Utah in 1948. In April 1950, Jennings edited and published the first number of a new monograph series *(University of Utah Anthropological Papers)*, with an article by Rudy and Stirland focusing on the archaeology of Washington County, Utah [251]. It was assigned number 9, and Jennings explained that numbers 1 to 8 would be reprints of out-of-print older University of Utah articles by Malouf, Dibble, Elmer Smith, Enger, and Tobin. Number 10, *The Archaeology of Deadman Cave*, by Elmer Smith [269] was declared "A Revision" of an earlier report.

The University of Utah surpassed all other Great Basin institutions in the quantity and quality of publications dealing with the archaeology of the Great Basin during the period, 1950–1975. Moreover, Utah rivaled the University of California in its record for research and publication regarding prehistory during the last quarter century. Utah's *Anthropological Papers* have reached ninety-five numbers. *Median Village and Fremont Culture Regional Variation* by J. P. Marwitt [189], number 95 in the series, takes issue with the commonplace view that Fremont Culture is an extension of the Puebloid Culture of the Southwest. Marwitt reviewed and correlated data establishing five Fremont variations in Utah which he named and plotted on a map: 1—Uinta; 2—San Rafael; 3—Great Salt Lake; 4—Sevier; 5—Parawan. Forty-one radio-carbon dates and eleven dates from dendrochronology (tree ring dating) have been determined from material taken at forty-six Fremont sites. The Great Salt Lake Fremont variation provided dates extending from 420 A.D. to 1310 A.D. The others varied from 520 A.D. to 1260 A.D., demonstrating variability and marked differences between Fremont cultures and Puebloid cultures as well as variances within Fremont Culture itself.

Between *Anthropological Paper No. 9,* regarding the prehistory of extreme southwestern Utah, and *No. 95,* which covered the entire state, the University of Utah published in its anthropological series sixty archaeological monographs, thirty-one of which concerned the salvage operations preceding the construction of the Glen Canyon Dam. When completed in 1963, this dam flooded streams along the southeastern edge of the Great Basin. Two other reports from Utah dealt with the very center of the Great Basin and have become classics for the prehistory of the area. These are *Danger Cave* and *Hogup Cave.*

Danger Cave by Jesse D. Jennings was simultaneously published as Memoir 17 of the Society for American Archaeology and as University of Utah Anthropological Papers No. 27 [126]. Danger Cave is on the Nevada-Utah border and is important because of the length of its occupancy: 9000 B.C. to 20 A.D. according to carbon-dating. In this impressive site, 1,872 complete flint artifacts and an additional 796 fragments were recovered. Specimens of pottery, wood, bone, grass, shell, basketry, hide, cordage, and other evidence of material culture were also found. The culture changed relatively little over the 9,000 year span of occupancy and fits nicely in the "Desert Culture" as defined by Jennings and Norbeck in their conceptual article, "Great Basin Prehistory: A Review" [129].

Hogup Cave, by C. Melvin Aikens [3], provides a marvelous comparison and enlargement of the prehistoric picture sketched by Jennings in *Danger Cave.* Hogup cave is just forty miles across sterile salt flats from Danger Cave. The cultures of the two are distinctive in some ways, yet they shared the same general culture patterns and time periods—6400 B.C to 1850 A.D. Aikens has also written a useful summary of prehistory in "The Far West," a chapter of Jennings' textbook, *Ancient Native Americans* [5].

Because of its more far-reaching theoretical proposition Jennings and Norbeck's "Great Basin Prehistory: A Review" [129] is as important as a by-product of the Danger Cave excavation as the actual artifacts recovered. Jennings and Norbeck, then colleagues at the University of Utah, placed knowledge from Danger Cave in context with other data regarding Great Basin prehistory. The concept they propounded is that there has existed a Desert Culture in the Great Basin that has had a general uniformity and continuity for at least 11,000 years. Slight differences occurred allowing the time to be divided into three culture periods: I—Desert Culture-Peripheral Big Game hunting; II—Desert Culture-Horticulture; III—Historic Desert Culture. Jennings and Norbeck recognized the extension of Desert Culture to Birdshead Cave in central Wyoming, where Basin-like rabbit skin "cloth," fiber cordage and grinding stones were found by Bliss [17].

In Birdshead Cave the excavators found steatite vessels which have also been uncovered in association with Shoshoni pottery elsewhere on the northern fringe of the Great Basin [345].

The impact of Jesse Jennings on Great Basin anthropology may have been greatest because of his textbooks. The earliest of these appeared in 1965 as *The Native Americans*, edited by Jennings and Spencer [127]. In the section entitled "Prehistory", Jennings reviewed the information available on Folsom Culture, Desert Culture and other Great Basin manifestations. More important was *Prehistory of North America* [128], first published in 1968. This has been adopted coast to coast for introductory courses in American archaeology. The prehistory of the Great Basin is well covered and placed in context with that of the remainder of tthe New World. Most recently Jennings has edited an excellent anthology on North and South American prehistory. *Ancient Native Americans* [130] is an important book for scholar and student alike and is a good update of knowledge of the First Americans.

Although there are many more important archaeological publications on the Great Basin, the titles listed cover the field and provide a sampling of data on the human occupations of the Great Basin from about 9000 B.C. to 1800 A.D.

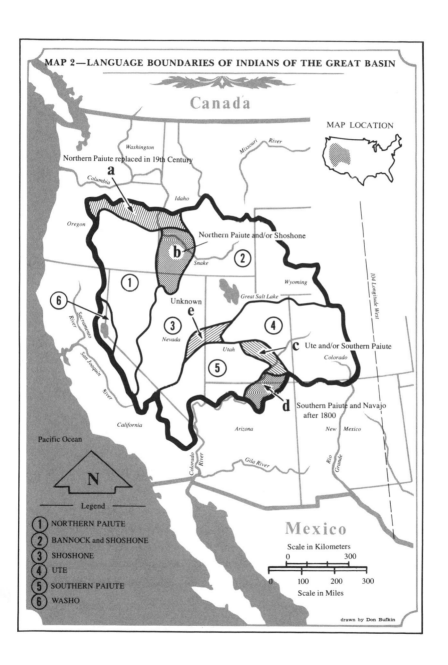

MAP 2—LANGUAGE BOUNDARIES OF INDIANS OF THE GREAT BASIN

Ethnology

The Great Basin Indians were included in the writings of the first American anthropologists, Henry Rowe Schoolcraft [256], Lewis Henry Morgan [212], and John Wesley Powell [236]. The next generation of American anthropologists, who wrote about the Indians of the Great Basin, as represented by Alfred L. Kroeber, Edward Sapir, J. Alden Mason and Robert H. Lowie, accepted the obligation to record the language, mythology, music, art, rules of behavior and ways of survival as remembered by the Indians themselves.

Robert H. Lowie must be honored as the first, if not the only "complete ethnographer" of the Great Basin tribes. Like his contemporaries listed above, except Powell, Lowie was more or less "sent" to the Great Basin by his professor at Columbia University, Franz Boas. In 1906 he went to the Lemhi Shoshoni; in 1912 to the Wind River Shoshonis and the Utes; in 1914 to the Northern Paiutes; in 1915 to the Southern Paiutes; and, in 1926 to the Washoes. His publications dealing with the Numic speakers and Washoe, scattered completely across the Great Basin east to west, and a little beyond, appeared from 1909 to 1939. These contributions represent field work extending over twenty years and publication stretched out for thirty years, plus one posthumous note on "Washo Texts" [175]. Yet, Lowie was best known for his studies of the Crows of Montana and the tribes of the Great Plains, and for his role as professor of anthropology at Berkeley from 1921 to

1953. Anthropologists trained at Berkeley who have carried on his interest in the Great Basin include most of the next generation of Basin ethnographers: Julian Steward, Isabel Kelly, Grace Dangberg, Cora DuBois, Willard Z. Park, Omer Stewart, Demitri Shimkin, Warren d'Azevedo, and Stanley and Ruth Freed. Although some of Lowie's students have continued the ethnographic methods pioneered by Lowie, with great interests in mythology, for example, others have become more concerned with acculturation of modern Indians.

UTES

Were we to use the recent linguistic classifications of the speech of the Great Basin, the Utes and Southern Paiutes would be combined as the Southern Numic [147]. Although speaking the same language (as Spanish and Portuguese are linguistically one), for a couple of centuries Utes and Southern Paiutes have been culturally separate from one another. Since 1776 when they were visited by the Spanish explorer, Escalante, the Utes from Central Utah to western Colorado have recognized their close affinity, but Escalante recorded a break between the Utes and Southern Paiutes [19].

The eastern Utes were the first Numic speakers to become acquainted with Spanish explorers and settlers. According to S. Lyman Tyler in his doctoral dissertation, "Before Escalante; an Early History of the Yuta

Indians and the Area North of New Mexico" [322], this first contact between Europeans and Utes occured before 1680. Tyler reproduced some of his historic evidence and interpretation in a number of articles, and his documentary research led him to publish "a bibliographic checklist" entitled *The Ute People* [325].

Although Utes came to be known as Northern Utes and Southern Utes following the removal of the White River and Uncompaghre Utes from Colorado to the Uintah Reservation in Utah after the Meeker Massacre in 1879, until that year the real division was between the eastern Utes of Colorado and the western Utes of Utah. No ethnographic study of the Utes, except word lists and mythology collected by Powell [60], preceded the Uncompaghre-White River removal; subsequently, ethnographers combined as "Northern Utes" the Uintah Ute from the vicinity of Utah Lake and the eastern Utes from Colorado because they were living side by side on the Uintah-Ouray Reservation in Utah.

The Utes were ethnologically classified as "Plains Indians" by early American anthropologists because of the historic reputation of the Utes as mounted horsemen raiding into the Great Plains and because of their reputation as respected enemies of the Kiowas, Cheyennes, Arapahoes, Sioux, and Comanches, when these Plains tribes were first interviewed by ethnographers. But the Utes retained basically a Great Basin culture, even after the adoption of horses which allowed them to hunt buffalo on the Plains and transport meat and hides back into or over the Rocky Mountains to their traditional territories. The eastern Utes were probably the most important Indians in the spread of the horse from the Spanish settlements to northern tribes because they had learned horsemanship as slaves of Spaniards before 1680. During the Pueblo Revolt they acquired herds of horses and quickly integrated them into their culture. These horses were driven along the western slope of the Rockies in present-day Colorado by the Utes to their linguistic kinsmen in Wyoming. The ideal horse pastures of Wyoming, Idaho and Washington were soon populated with herds of horses because of the knowledge of animal husbandry passed along by the Utes with the horses to other tribes. Francis Haines [81] [82] in his often-quoted articles on the spread of the horse indicated on his maps that the horses went to Idaho via central Utah. This would have been very difficult given the topography along Haine's route of diffusion and is contradicted by Spanish reports from the mid-eighteenth century [19].

The first general ethnography of the Utes was based on the eastern Utes of Colorado and appeared as "The Southern Ute Indians," by Verner Z. Reed [244]. Reed also wrote about Ute chiefs [245] and the Ute Bear Dance [246].

Robert Lowie's *Notes on Shoshonean Ethnography* [173] and his monograph on mythology, "Shoshonean Tales" [172], included considerable data on the Utes and remained the primary ethnographic source on the Utes until the appearance of reports by Marvin K. Opler and Omer C. Stewart. Opler's study was based on field work in 1936 and 1937, under the direction of Professor Ralph Linton. He followed an outline supplied by Linton to analyze acculturation and published his study, "The Southern Ute of Colorado" in Linton's anthology, *Acculturation in Seven American Indian Tribes* [225]. Additional articles on such subjects as the Bear Dance [227], Sun Dance [228], Dog Dance [223], Origins [230], and Peyote Religion [226] [229] by Opler have appeared in various journals.

Doing field work on the Uintah-Ouray Reservation in Utah in 1936 and 1937, Anne M. Cooke Smith collected data for a master's thesis, "The Material Culture of the Northern Ute," [266], and a doctoral dissertation completed in 1939 as "An Analysis of Basin Mythology" [267]. The academic community is rewarded because Anne Smith kept her field notes for nearly forty years and also guarded field notes and photographs entrusted to her by Edward Sapir. Her monograph, *Ethnography of the Northern Utes* [268] is enriched by twenty-three photographs taken in 1909, in addition to her own visuals.

Omer Stewart's principle ethnographic contribution is his publication "Culture Element Distributions: XVIII, Ute—Southern Paiute" [293]. Directed by A. L. Kroeber at the University of California at Berkeley, the Culture Element Survey was carried out by means of short visits to almost every Indian group in the western United States. Julian Steward and Omer Stewart visited all of the Great Basin groups with a basic list of over 4000 culture elements arranged systematically in chart form so that presence or absence of the elements could be recorded, and then supplemental notes could be appended whenever needed. All questions were asked by Stewart of old informants representing three aboriginal Ute groups from central Utah and four from Colorado. Although an unorthodox method for recording ethnographic data, the Ute "element-list" preserves a large quantity of information which would be lost otherwise.

During the Culture Element Survey, Stewart had an opportunity to attend meetings of the Native American Church in Utah and Colorado which started an interest in Peyotism [292] that has continued to the present [306]. His first major study, *Ute Peyotism* [295], included a comparison of the Ute ritual with other Native American peyote usage. Although completed before the Second World War, that conflict delayed publication until 1948. Therefore, Stewart brought his study up to date in a 1957 publication with David Arberle entitled *Navaho and Ute Peyotism: A Chronological and Distributional Study* [1].

Because religious ceremonies represent that part of modern Ute culture which appears to preserve an aboriginal flavor, they have received much attention. For example, the Ute Bear Dance, a spring festival that may be as much a courting ritual as one of worship, has been in the title of articles by Reed [246], Reagan [241], Steward [276], Monaghan [197], Karl Young [362] and Marvin Opler [227]. Furthermore, important sections were devoted to the Ute Bear Dance in publications by

Lowie [170], Densmore [43], Stewart [293], Jorgenson [134], Jefferson, et al. [125], and Anne Smith [268].

A short ethnological study of the Ute Sun Dance was presented by Lowie [171], and the Sun Dance was described by Marvin Opler [225] [228], Omer Stewart [293], Young [363], and Anne Smith [268]. What is probably the definitive publication on the subject is *The Sun Dance Religion: Power for the Powerless* by Joseph G. Jorgensen [134]. This is an angry book designed to expose the exploitation of Great Basin Indians by the dominant White population and to propose that the Sun Dance serves to help the Indians endure. Based primarily on the Ute, it also includes in its long description and comparative table the dances of the Fort Hall and Wind River Shoshonis.

John A. Jones wrote on the Sun Dance for a doctoral thesis at Columbia University. This was rewritten for publication as Bureau of American Ethnology Bulletin 157 [133] with the title *The Sun Dance of the Northern Ute*.

Subsequent to the ethnographic research of the 1930s and the reports flowing from it, nearly all publications dealing with modern Utes, except studies of Ute language, can be characterized under the heading of "acculturation." Most also are dependent upon historical documents, and thus could be called ethnohistorical. The first report by Gottfried O. Lang, entitled *A Study in Culture Contact and Culture Change: The Whiterock Utes in Transition* [154] consisted primarily of a summary of the results of a socio-economic survey conducted in 1950 and is a useful beginning for readers interested in culture change. Lang submitted "The Ute Development Program" for his doctorate [155] and he has published articles on acculturation on the Unintah-Ouray Reservation. Thomas W. Collins has continued the research of modern Northern Ute initiated by Lang. His dissertation, "The Northern Ute Economic Development Program: Social and Cultural Dimensions" [30] is an important study of the impact of twentieth-century economic programs. Another study in acculturation was completed by Younger T. Witherspoon in 1961 and deals with "Cultural Influences on Ute Learning" [355]. In the same category is the article entitled "The Reluctant Suzerainty: The Uintah-Ouray Reservation," by Floyd A. O'Neil [222]. Stewart's "Ute Indians: Before and After White Contact" [301] outlines changes and retentions in Ute cultural history.

In 1977 the Uintah-Ouray Ute Tribe published five books of various aspects of their culture and history. *A Brief History of the Ute People* [328], *The Ute People* [329], *Ute Ways* [330], *The Way It Was Told* [331], and *The Ute System of Government* [332] are representative of a refreshing trend among Indian tribes to write their own studies and make them available for the general public. All are recommended for the beginner and should be acquired for a well-rounded basic library on the Ute people.

Tribal histories have in part been the result of the Duke Oral Indian History Project under the direction of C. Gregory Crampton, at the University of Utah, who began collecting Ute myths, legends, and personal histories by means of taped recordings. Ute Indian college students assisted in the recordings and translated from Ute to English where required. Two volumes have been compiled from this material: *Ute People: An Historical Study* [176] by June Lyman and Norman Denver dealt with the Uintah-Ouray Reservation; *The Southern Utes: A Tribal History* [125] by Jefferson, Delaney and Thompson emphasized Colorado. Delaney and Thompson are White professional historians who contributed a large ethnohistorical section. The Southern Ute Tribe paid for the publication and has charge of its distribution. Other Ute tribal documents are published as annual reports and proposed programs, and as news items in the two weekly papers published by the tribe: *The Southern Ute Drum*, Ignacio, Colorado; and *The Ute Bulletin*, Fort Duchesne, Utah.

Among the Colorado Utes, recent anthropological research—except in linguistics—has been oriented to modern adjustment, building upon the research originally initiated by Marvin K. Opler. "Southern Ute Adjustment to Modern Living," by Omer C. Stewart [296], is a preliminary report on a community study of the reservation town of Ignacio, Colorado. Carried on intermittently from 1948 to 1975, the research beame identified as the Tri-ethnic Project because Spanish and Anglo members of the community were investigated along with the Ute Indians. A number of doctoral dissertations grew out of that research: Langner [156],

Graves [73], Johnson [132], Stevens [274], Swadesh [308], Hoyt [108], and Tyzzer [326].

The principle results of the Tri-ethnic project research, financed from 1959 to 1964 by grants from the National Institute of Mental Health, were published as *Society, Personality, and Deviant Behavior*, by Richard Jessor, Theodore D. Graves, Robert C. Hanson, and Shirley I. Jessor [131]. Another book from the Tri-ethnic Project is *Los Primeros Pobladores* by Frances Leon Swadesh [309], which focuses on the Hispanos of Ignacio and their history. Omer C. Stewart's *Ethnohistorical Bibliography of the Ute Indians of Colorado* [303] is another by-product of this five-year project.

SOUTHERN PAIUTES

Chemehuevis are culturally and linguisticly Southern Paiutes who have lived during historic times on both sides of the Colorado River near present-day Lake Havasu City, Arizona, and in Chemehuevi Valley and the Mohave Desert of California. A. L. Kroeber's substantial reference work, *Handbook of the Indians of California* [148], provides the basic information about the Chemehuevi and also the Kawaiisu, an offshoot to the west. John Wesley Powell collected myths of the Southern Paiute [60] as did Edward Sapir [253]. Isabel T. Kelly's *Southern Paiute Ethnography* [140] and four important articles [136] [137] [138] [139] provide the primary data on the Southern Paiutes. In his culture element survey, Stewart recorded data from four Southern Paiute bands to compare and contrast with information from seven Ute bands [293]. The Inter-Tribal Council of Nevada, in cooperation with the Southern Paiute Tribe, has published *NUWUVI* [117], a tribal history of the Southern Paiutes. Also of note is Carobeth Laird's recent monograph, *The Chemehuevi* [150], the most complete source on this little known group.

Both Steward [283] and Fowler [57] reproduced photographs of the Southern Paiutes taken by Hiller while on the Powell expedition, 1871–1875, and Fowler edited Hiller's diary. Robert C. Euler in *Southern Paiute Ethnohistory* [51] brought together material from most of the historic references to the group, and Euler's *The Paiute People* [52] is a popular summary of Southern Paiute culture.

The basis for the conflict between the two tribal groups speaking the Southern Numic language is set forth by Carling and A. A. Malouf in their article, "The Effects of Spanish Slavery on the Indians of the Intermountain West" [185] which presents the evidence that Ute Indians captured Southern Paiute children and sold them to the Spaniards.

Recent material consists of a dissertation entitled "Contemporary Southern Paiute Household Structure and Bilateral Kinship Clusters" by Martha C. Knack [142] and *Kaibab Paiute History: The Early Years* by Richard W. Stoffle and Michael J. Evans [307]. Stoffle has a long-range project which will certainly produce publications concerning his work with the Southern Paiutes to help them develop more income from their reservation in the "Arizona Strip" near Kanab, Utah.

SHOSHONIS

The Shoshoni Indians occupied the largest and most diverse territory of the Numic speakers of the Great Basin. Shoshonis utilized land varying in elevation from Death Valley (282 feet below sea level) to the summit of the Wind River Range in the Rocky Mountains of Wyoming, which rise over 13,000 feet above sea level. Although the Shoshonis lived on the banks of Snake River in Idaho, that river was generally entrenched and afforded little chance for valley and riverine flora to take hold. The Snake River Plains were, therefore, semi-arid to arid and were covered with desert shrubs. Western Wyoming, western Utah and Nevada, also part of Shoshonis' territory, were a similar environment. The Great Salt Lake and the Great Salt Lake Desert comprised the final region of Shoshoni-occupied territory.

Although colonial Spanish explorers did not enter Shoshoni country, according to the map drawn by Miera showing the route of Escalante through Ute territory, Shoshoni camps are depicted under the name "Cumanchis" in what would be western Wyoming and in Utah west of Utah Lake. This map, published by Bolton in his *Pageant in the Wilderness* [19], is a reminder that the Comanches, most famous for their warfare in Oklahoma, Texas and Mexico, were at one time Shoshonis of the Great Basin.

The Shoshonis, known first as "Snakes," were reported as mounted raiders in Canada and North Dakota before the American explorers, Lewis and Clark hired a Shoshoni woman, Sacajawea, and her husband to be interpreters for the expedition of the Pacific in 1805–06. Grace Hebard's *Sacajawea* [90] is an interpretation of this famous Shoshoni woman's importance in guiding and serving as liaison for Lewis and Clark. Reuben Gold Thwaites's edition of the *Original Journals of the Lewis and Clark Expedition, 1804–1806* [319] has at least fifty references to Shoshonis in eight volumes. A useful index will lead the researcher to information regarding Shoshoni interaction with the explorers.

Thwaites also edited thirty-two volumes of primary travel accounts under the title, *Early Western Travels, 1748–1846* [318]. This rich collection of narratives has an excellent index in volumes 31–32. References to Shoshonis are contained in the accounts of Thomas Jefferson Farnham, John Long, John K. Townsend, Nathaniel Jarvis Wyeth, James Ohio Pattie, and Joel Palmer. Wyeth also wrote a report for Henry Rowe Schoolcraft's 1853 publication, *Historical and Statistical Information . . .* [256] and mentioned several Great Basin tribes. Other fur trappers and traders who wrote enough about Shoshonis to justify examination of their published accounts were Alexander Ross [250], Osborne Russell [252], and Warren A. Ferris [53].

Many ethnographers have made significant contributions to historical and cultural studies of the Shoshonis. Robert Lowie's three major works on the tribe are the essential starting point for any researcher. His "The Northern Shoshone" [169], *Shoshonean Tales* [172], and *Notes on Shoshonean Ethnography* [173], produced between 1909 and 1924, remained practically the only sources for almost three decades on that neglected language group. His student, Julian H. Steward, changed that situation with three monographs of his own, *Basin-Plateau Aboriginal Sociopolitical Groups* [282], *Northern and Gosiute Shoshoni* [286], and *Nevada Shoshone* [285]. Steward visited most of the surviving Shoshoni populations from Death Valley to Fort Hall, Idaho. The results of his field research and analysis of most of the historic documents about the area were summarized and used to support his theories in his widely acclaimed book, *Theory of Culture Change* [287].

Steward's work on Shoshonean cultural adaptations to the Great Basin and his pioneering testing of quantification of culture-elements while working with Indians of the Basin in the 1930s produced a new understanding of Shoshoni socio-economic structure, and by implication, that of most cultures of the province. Steward theorized that the family-band level of sociocultural integration was the key to various Indians' successful adjustment to the harsh environment of the arid and semi-arid regions of the Far West. Although his own work did not verify the theory, Steward's view became widely accepted until the 1960s when Elman R. Service, Omer Stewart, and Roger Owen questioned

Steward's upstreaming of data from the 1930s to explain aboriginal social organization.

Service in his *Primitive Social Organization* [257] and Owen in the "The Patrilocal Band: A Linguistically and Culturally Hybrid Social Unit" [231] suggested that the basic unit of the prehistoric Great Basin was not Steward's "family band," but rather the "patrilocal band." According to Service, the scattered Shoshonean families observed by Steward in the 1930s were merely the survivors of Great Basin peoples whose social and political organizations had been radically altered from their ancestors by White contact situations. Omer C. Stewart in "Tribal Distributions and Boundaries in the Great Basin" [300] challenged Steward regarding the territorial tendencies of the prehistoric Shoshonean-speakers, and more recently proposed that the "Oasis Concept" [306] suggests further questioning of Julian Steward's interpretations.

Recently David Hurst Thomas in "An Empirical Test for Steward's Model of Great Basin Settlement Patterns" [314] has used data collected in the Reese River Ecological Project to show at least one example where Steward's theory can be verified. Thomas did not claim Steward's theory to be fact after his own work bore out Steward's model, but it is an extremely important case study having broad implications for all of the Great Basin. Stated simply, Steward's theory implied that Great Basin cultural ecology had a socially fragmenting effect upon aboriginal populations. The constraints imposed by this harsh, unpredictable environment were such that traditional institutions other than the nuclear family were notably absent. Ecological relationships predetermined the population density, limited the size, mobility and distribution of village groups, and influenced the overall nature of economic cooperation and property rights. Shoshonis depended upon a multiple subsistence pattern which exploited contiguous but dissimilar microenvironments. Plants were the staple foods of the pattern, with piñon nuts and hard-shelled seeds from herbaceous plants being the most important wild crops. Under this system there was sufficient plant food so long as people dispersed in groups of only a few families. Hunting was a secondary activity to supplement the essentially vegetal diet.

Residence and demographic patterns centered about a semi-permanent winter village encampment. These villages accommodated fifteen to twenty families and were located so that the Shoshonis could maximize diversity in their subsistence rounds. Ideal village sites were situated between the sagebrush flats and the piñon-juniper belt flanking the mountains. According to Steward, the ideal conditions for winter camps were accessibility to stored seeds (especially pine nuts), water, sufficient wood for house building and fuel, and absence of extremely low winter temperatures. During winter, families cooperated in the hunting of jack rabbits and antelope. During the summers family units left the winter camp to reestablish habitation closer to the ripening herbaceous plants. If piñon harvests were sufficient within a small distance from the winter camp, the family band units stayed close to the semi-permanent winter village. If the harvest was poor they fanned out farther, returning to the winter camp in the fall.

Other Lowie students have produced major contributions focusing on the Shoshonis. Demitri Shimkin wrote his doctoral dissertation, "Some Interactions of Culture, Needs, and Personalities among the Wind River Shoshone" [258], and three studies of Wind River Shoshonis, the section of that tribal group Steward had not visited. These were: "Childhood and Development among the Wind River Shoshone" [259], "Wind River Shoshone Ethnogeography" [260], and "Wind River Shoshone Sun Dance" [261]. He also wrote several articles, including two on Shoshonean linguistics. Next to Lowie and his students, the most productive scholar writing about the Shoshonis is Åke Hultkrantz of Stockholm, Sweden. From 1951 to 1966 he wrote twelve articles on that band of Shoshonis who subsisted by hunting mountain sheep and who lived in the highest mountains of Yellowstone Park and south into the Tetons and Wind River Range. "The Origin of Death Myth as Found among the Wind River Shoshoni Indians" [112] and "Configurations of Religious Belief among the Wind River Shoshoni" [113] are the most important of these articles. Hultkrantz's general article, "The Shoshone in the Rocky Mountain Area" [114], is very valuable as an overview.

Robert F. and Yolanda Murphy did an ethnohistorical report for the United States Department of Justice and it was placed in evidence in the Shoshoni Claims Case. Later it was published as "Shoshone-Bannock Subsistence and Society" [214].

The Sun Dance of the Shoshonis was described and compared with the Plains Sun Dance by Lowie [171] and was the foundation of a book by Jorgensen [134] which also covered the Utes. Fred W. Voget wrote his doctoral dissertation on the Wind River Shoshoni Sun Dance [337] and used data on the subject for articles on "Individual Motivation" [338], "A Shoshone Innovator" [339] and "Current Trends in the Wind River Shoshone Sun Dance" [340]. E. Adamson Hoebel [101] described the Sun Dance of the Shoshonis of Idaho.

"The Peyote Cult among Wyoming Indians" by Molly Stenberg [273] devoted most of the space to the Shoshonis. An acculturation study by Jack Harris, "The White Knife Shoshone of Nevada" [86], remains one of the longest reports of a single Western Shoshoni group. It is comparable to the monograph, *The Gosiute Indians,* by Carling Malouf [183], who also wrote an article on "Gosiute Peyotism" [184].

The Shoshoni Indians of Idaho have been intermixed with the Northern Paiute-speaking Bannocks since at least 1819 when Alexander Ross, an employee of the Hudson Bay Company, reported them on the Snake River plain [250]. In the article, "The Question of Bannock Territory" [302], Stewart cited 68 reports of Shoshonis and Bannocks traveling or camping together from 1819 to 1956. Stewart also wrote the section on "The Shoshone of the Great Basin" [298] in the popular text book, *The Native Americans*. His "The Shoshoni: Their History and Social Organization" [299] proposes that the Shoshoni developed a class system when they obtained horses. Sven Liljeblad wrote *Indian Peoples of Idaho* [166] providing much information on the interrelations of Bannocks and Shoshonis. Brigham D. Madsen's *The Bannock of Idaho* [179] is a good history of that tribe and contains coverage of the Shoshonis as well. Madsen made it clear that the two had to be considered together. A less professional book, with many errors, is *The Shoshonis: Sentinels of the Rockies* by Virginia Trenholm and Maurine Carley [317]. They cited a great number of historic and anthropological sources but could not properly evaluate the material quoted. Much of their data came from Dale L. Morgan's "Washakie and the Shoshoni" [204], a series of articles which appeared in *Annals of Wyoming* from 1954 to 1958. A remarkable history of the Shoshoni is now recommended as a classic for juvenile readers, but has value for all: *The White Indian Boy* by E. N. Wilson [353] is the story of Shoshoni life in Wyoming, Idaho, and Utah, for about a decade after 1854 when Wilson, as a boy of twelve, left home and lived with the tribe. Although completed years later, the book is a very important eyewitness account of Shoshoni life in the late nineteenth century.

Another amateur historian, Edna B. Patterson, of Elko, Nevada, interviewed old Shoshoni shamans and wrote a very instructive book, *Sagebursh Doctors* [234].

Mrs. Patterson also collaborated with Louisa A. Ulph and Victor Goodwin in *Nevada's Northeast Frontier* [233] and devoted considerable space to the Shoshonis in the region covered. Two final publications of importance are *NEWW: A Western Shoshone History* [115] published by the Intertribal Council of Nevada and Deward Walker, *Indians of Idaho* [343].

NORTHERN PAIUTES

Since 1873 differences of opinion have existed concerning the correct name for the Indians most recently designated as speaking Western Numic by Wick R. Miller [193]. The Indians of western Nevada were designated Pah-Utah or Py-Utes as early as 1844. In 1873 Powell [236] insisted that "Paviotso" be used for Northern Paiutes to distinguish them from the Southern Paiutes of extreme southern Nevada and Utah. Most authors writing of the Indians of western Nevada and southeastern Oregon during the last half-century have used the name Northern Paiute, but Paviotso persists, for example, in the *Ethnographic Bibliography of North America* by Murdock and O'Leary [213]. Of the 95 titles under Paviotso listed by Murdock and O'Leary thirty-six authors used Northern Paiute, and only seven wrote "Paviotso." Two used the two names alternately.

The early date of publication and honored status of some of the writers on the Northern Paiutes render this Great Basin tribe better known than many of its neighbors. For example, Powell [236] recorded their myths, collected vocabularies, and a "List of Northern Paiute Chiefs," as his manuscript MS810 was titled. Great notoriety came to the Northern Paiutes in 1883 by means of the book, *Life Among the Piutes,* by Sarah Winnemucca Hopkins [102], the daughter of the most famous Northern Paiute Chief, Winnemucca. Sarah had traveled from coast to coast lecturing on the plight of her people and in Boston she attracted Mrs. Horace Mann to edit and copy a large manuscript for use by printers. The book has been reproduced and is a required source book for Northern Paiute ethnography.

Of more enduring fame was another, slightly younger Northern Paiute with the native name of Wovoka, who had been named Jack Wilson by the farmer on whose land he lived. Wovoka was a medicine man whose ritual for a world renewal ceremony became known to Plains tribes and the world as the Ghost Dance of 1890. James Mooney's report [198] has been the ultimate source on the subject. Mooney interviewed Wovoka and used contemporary documents made available within months of the Wounded Knee Massacre. Paul Bailey wrote a popular history of Wovoka and interpreted events of his life from Wounded Knee until his death in 1932 in his *Wovoka: The Indian Messiah* [11]. Grace Dangberg edited "Letters to Jack Wilson, The Paiute Prophet" [35].

Anthropological theorizing about Wovoka and his Ghost Dance has been complicated by the discovery that there was also a Ghost Dance in 1870 with many features similar to the one of 1890. The monograph of Cora Du Bois [47] is the major source for data on the manifestations of 1870. The ceremony has been reconsidered in the "The 1870 Ghost Dance at the Walker River Reservation: A Reconstruction" by Michael Hittman [98]. A short report of 1917 by a Bureau of Indian Affairs inspector denied that Wovoka was a link between the Ghost Dance and the Peyote religion which was declared illegal in Nevada that year. The official report mentioned a photograph of Wovoka, which was found in the National Archives and published by Omer Stewart [304].

Northern Paiute religion has repeatedly attracted attention since the passing of Wovoka. Joe Green, a medicine man of the Pyramid Lake Paiute Reservation, was the major informant for *Shamanism in Western North America* by Willard Z. Park [232] and was the star in Stewart's article, "Three Gods for Joe" [297], which documented that Joe was at the same time a shaman (medicine man), a believer in Peyotism, and a Deacon in the Episcopal mission. Stewart's doctoral dissertation of "Washo-Northern Paiute Peyotism" [294] was published by the University of California in their *Publications in Archaeology and Ethnology* series. Since the 1940s Stewart has continued his research on the Native American Church in the Great Basin. Michael Hittman's dissertation, "Ghost Dances, Disillusionment and Opiate Addition: An Ethnohistory of Smith and Mason Valley Paiutes" [99] should also be examined.

Other early writers on Northern Paiute ethnography deserve citing. The first is Stephen Powers who was commissioned in 1875 by Powell to make a report and collect objects of Indian manufacture on "the eastern slope of the Sierras" for the Centennial Exhibition in Philadelphia. Powers' major publication was *Tribes of California* [238] which included a section on the Northern Paiute of Owens Valley. Powers's "The Life and Culture of the Washo and Paiutes" [59] [237], based on his visits of 1875 to Northern Paiute Indians at Pyramid Lake, Walker Lake, and Honey Lake and the Washoes near Carson City, Nevada, remained unpublished until 1970. In that twenty page article, Powers made a reference to the Southern Paiutes in Inyo County, California. It is remarkable that the ethnographic data collected in 1875 should agree so closely with those collected by Stewart in 1936 [291].

C. Hart Merriam is another important student of the Northern Paiute whose collected data remained unpublished for decades. From 1900 to 1942 Merriam visited tribes on both flanks of the Sierra Nevada range in California. On the eastern side of the Sierras he traveled among the Northern Paiutes who were in both California and Nevada. Merriam consulted many of the historic accounts of visitors—official and lay—who mentioned the groups by name and made lists of names and locations by dates. His *Studies of California Indians* [191], published in 1955, contained listings of the various terms for historical Paiutes. He found that "Pah-Utes" or "Piutes" had been recorded eighty times from 1841 to 1923. An important variation was "Pa-

hutes of the North", used by the Spaniard Don Pablo
Belarde, in 1844. Merriam discovered that Powell used
both "Pah-Ute" and "Paviotso" for the same people.
Merriam's special contributions are his many clear and
detailed photographs of near-aboriginal living conditions of the Northern Paiutes in the early 1900s. He
photographed Northern Paiute summer and winter
dwellings and several types of baskets. In 1903 he photographed a Pyramid Lake Paiute winter house in the
process of construction and later one already completed, thus providing an excellent source for understanding more of daily life and material culture.

C. Hart Merriam and Edward S. Curtis were contemporaries and are both celebrated for their photographs of the Northern Paiute and Washo Indians,
among others. Curtis was a professional photographer
and only named his research assistants without iden-
tifying their contributions. All of the texts regarding
the Northern Paiutes and Washoes could have been
written by Curtis or his researchers. Although Curtis
published portfolios and books of photographs from
1907 to 1930, with volume 15 containing Great Basin
material [33], popular appreciation of his great contribution did not develop until the 1960s and 1970s.

The text of *The North American Indians,* a massive
twenty volume set subsidized by J. Pierpont Morgan,
with introductions by President Theodore Roosevelt,
was written in a popular romantic literary style without
footnotes and with few bibliographic references. Anthropologists find little useful information in the twenty

volumes although the photographs have intrinsic documentary, as well as aesthetic, value and have been frequently reprinted.

Robert Lowie included Northern Paiutes in his *Notes on Shoshonean Ethnography* [173], but the best modern ethnographic studies of the North Paiutes started with Kelly and her "Ethnography of the Surprise Valley Paiute" [136].

Surprise Valley was the country of the Northern Paiutes in California north of Lake Tahoe; Owens Valley remains territory of the Northern Paiutes in California south of Lake Tahoe. Steward's research on the Owens Valley Paiutes [278] is comparable to that of Kelly for the Surprise Valley Paiutes. A similar single-group ethnography was written by Beatrice Whiting. In *Paiute Sorcery* [350] she exhaustively describes the shamanism of the Harney Valley, Oregon, band of Northern Paiutes. There follows a comparison of Paiute sorcery with that of fifty tribes picked from the Human Relations Area Files. Supplementing the study of sorcery are ten pages of ethnographic notes similar to the data recorded for the Surprise Valley Paiutes by Kelly. No other traditional ethnographies of Northern Paiutes have been published.

Based primarily on the monographs of Steward and Kelly, Ruth M. Underhill wrote a pamphlet, *The Northern Paiute Indians of California and Nevada* [327], which was intended especially for teachers in Indian schools in Northern Paiute country, but which has proved valuable for general education about the Indians of the western edge of the Great Basin and has been regularly reprinted.

The Cultural Element Distribution studies of the Northern Paiutes were carried on by Julian Steward and Omer Stewart. In *Nevada Shoshone* [285], Steward included data on three Northern Paiute groups, two from Owens Valley and one from Mill City, Nevada. Using the same list of culture-elements Stewart [291] recorded data from eleven Northern Paiute groups, which Stewart designated as bands. These were more fully defined in a separate publication, "The Northern Paiute Bands" [290]. The bands discussed by Stewart had occupied the territory from Hawthorne, Nevada, north to Burns, Oregon, and from Surprise Valley, California to the region of Idaho-Oregon border in extreme southwestern Idaho. Thus Stewart's lists were recorded for the same bands studied by Kelly [136] and Whiting [350].

Stewart supplemented his own ethnographic data with a thorough search of historical documents in order to serve as an expert witness for the Northern Paiutes before the United States Indian Claims Commission. Julian Steward testified for the Department of Justice in the same case and, with Erminie Wheeler-Voegelin, prepared a report, *The Northern Paiute Indians* [289]. Most of the Northern Paiute report prepared for the Department of Justice was also published in "The Northern Paiute of Central Oregon: A Chapter in Treaty-Making" by Wheeler-Voegelin [349].

Steward's interest in the question of whether or not

Northern Paiute "bands" should be considered as distinct socio-political groups contributed significantly to his last article, "The Foundations of Basin-Plateau Shoshonean Society" [288]. In the same volume Robert Heizer [92] and Shimkin and Reid [262] discuss two Northern Paiute bands first defined by Stewart in 1939 [290]. Margaret Wheat's *Survival Arts of the Primitive Paiutes* [348] is a well-illustrated reference work on Northern Paiute material culture.

Research on Northern Paiutes continues, but results vary. Modern problems and modern techniques have been the focus of several recent publications, many of which apply newer approaches to ancient problems. For example, focusing on the Owens Valley Paiutes, Bertram Roberts wrote a two-part article, "Descendants of the *Numu*" [248], the Paiute name for themselves. More sophisticated is Robert L. Bettinger's "Multivariate Statistical Analysis of a Regional Subsistence-Settlement Model for Owens Valley" [15]. James F. O'Connell's *The Prehistory of Surprise Valley* [218] is another example of a recent sophistocated interpretation of prehistoric subsistence and settlement patterns. Although the report is mainly concerned with the prehistory of the Northern Paiutes, the implications of the study are important for understanding ecological adaptation for all peoples of the Great Basin across time. Dividing his discussion into "lowland" and "upland" occupation sites, O'Connell demonstrates that Great Basin tribes successfully adjusted to changing climatic changes and variations in available resources

well before European contact. Historic tribes of the
province reflect a much older trend toward demo-
graphically smaller settlement units. O'Connell's work
on Paiute prehistory supports Steward's theories fo-
cused on the Shoshonis, in that at Surprise Valley the
principal social unit changed from extended families
living in permanent villages with earth lodges to nuclear families living in semi-permanent camps in lowland and upland portions of the culture area, depend-
ing on the season. In the camps, prehistoric Paiutes
built small domed wickiups and unroofed brush
windscreens. This major change in housing and in
demographic pattern was brought about by climatic
shifts from a cool-moist environment to a warm-dry
norm, characteristic of the Basin today. Quantity of
food consumed after permanent villages were aban-
doned seems to have remained consistent, although the
dispersal necessitated by the changes in precipitation
forced diversification of gathering activities while hunting remained a secondary subsistence industry.

On Pyramid Lake Paiutes, Alvin R. McLane produced an annotated bibliography of 541 titles [178].
Special studies of the group include Gomberg and Leland [69] on aspirations and talents. Pamela J. Brink
wrote a doctoral thesis on Pyramid Lake Paiute child
training [21], and summarized her findings in
"Paviotso Child Training: Notes" [22].

The Pyramid Lake water case, *United States vs.
Truckee-Carson Irrigation District et al.,* stimulated considerable ethnographic research and resulted in an article

by Martha C. Knack [143], and a book in preparation by Knack and Stewart [144]. Ruth M. Houghton completed her master's and doctoral theses on modern conditions on the McDermitt Paiute Indian Reservation [104] [105]. The Northern Paiutes continue to attract attention from ethnographers and their traditional territory continues to be of interest to archaeologists. In 1976 the Intertribal Council of Nevada sponsored publication of *NUMA: A Northern Paiute History* [116], essential reading for the beginner.

WASHOES

The Washoes have been of special interest to anthropology because of their unique geographic, cultural and linguistic position. Some Washoes occupied the high Sierra Mountain valleys near Sierraville and Loyalton, California, north of Lake Tahoe. The majority of the tribe lived during the summers around Lake Tahoe, but then descended to the valleys east of the mountains to spend the winter in the vicinity of modern Reno, Carson City and Gardnerville, Nevada. Washoe territory was better watered generally, than the other parts of the Great Basin and such a geographic advantage might have been responsible for the statistical difference discovered by Kroeber in 1957 [149] when he compared the cultures of the Washoes with that of the eleven Northern Paiute bands originally interviewed by Omer Stewart in 1941 [291]. By including Washoes in a research project covering the Northern Paiutes, Stewart, during the University of California "Element Survey", continued a practice started by Powers [238], repeated by Sarah Winnemucca [102] and again repeated by Stewart in his study of "Washo-Northern Paiute Peyotism" [294].

In view of the small population of 900 in 1859, according to Kroeber in 1925 [148], and "approximately 1,000 in 1959, in *Findings of Fact* of the Indian Claims Commission [335], studies of the Washoes have made a remarkable contribution to Great Basin anthropology. Kroeber devoted one of his early studies among California Indians to Washoe language [146], and then he described their culture in his *Handbook of Indians of California* [148]. The chapter on the Washoes and the beautiful photographs by Edward S. Curtis of the Washoe Indians and of the magnificient baskets of Dat-So-La-Lee [33], often judged the finest in the world, provide a literary and artistic supplement to Kroeber's scientific presentation.

Although not as artistic as those of Curtis, the photographs by S. A. Barrett [12] depict Washoe material culture, including aboriginal houses, stone and wood implements, and several styles of baskets *circa* 1917. Lowie [174] [175] produced a more traditional ethnography, including nineteen short myths and tales. Danberg [36] added several much longer myths.

The more recent ethnographic reports on the Washoes were completed by, or were associated with, Warren L. d'Azevedo, for many years an anthropologist at the University of Nevada. His edited work, *The Washo Indians of California and Nevada* [39], contains articles by the following authors who have produced other works also: Stanley A. Freed [61], John A. Price [239] [240], and James F. Downs [45] [46]. Warren d'Azevedo collaborated with Merriam on an important article entitled "Washo Peyote Songs" [190], which should be supplemented with Edgar Siskin's "The Impact of the Peyote Cult upon Shamanism among the Washo Indians" [265]. Modern and exhaustive studies of Washo language have been carried on by William H. Jacobsen, Jr. [124] and his students at the University of Nevada, Reno.

Maurice L. Zigmond [364] describes the G. A. Steiner Museum on the Kennedy Mill Farm, near Portersville, Pennsylvania, which houses sixty-four Washoe baskets and fifty-six from other Great Basin tribes among a unique collection of 555 American Indian baskets. The researcher interested in prehistoric baskets of the Great Basin will find J. M. Adovasio's article on that subject [2] of great interest. Those readers seeking a good introductory work on the Washoes should consult *WA SHE SHU: A Washo Tribal History* [118] in addition to the aforementioned works by James F. Downs [45] [46].

Linguistics

Vocabularies, the first materials for the study of languages, were collected by some of the earliest European travelers in the Great Basin. Ross [250] in 1824, Wyeth [361] in 1832, and Gebow [67] in 1864, were three early travelers who prepared vocabularies in Shoshoni. Fowler and Fowler [60] list Horatio Hale of the Wilkes expedition of 1838–1842 as the first recorder of Northern Paiute, and members of the Whipple expedition of 1856 as making vocabularies of Chemehuevi (Southern Paiute), Ute and other Numic languages in the south.

Powell recorded Numic vocabularies during his many trips to the Great Basin from 1868 to 1880. Linguistic texts of myths were also recorded and translated. One was written in Ute in Washington, D.C. with interlinear translation by Uintah Ute Richard Komas who was working for Powell as a clerk-interpreter in the Bureau of Ethnology from 1875 to 1877 [60].

Among the giants of American anthropology is Alfred L. Kroeber who, in 1900, at the age of twenty-four and while still a graduate student at Columbia University, collected vocabularies from Bannocks and Shoshonis at Fort Hall, Idaho and from Uintah Utes at Whiterocks, Utah. Other Numic vocabularies — Kawaiisu, Paviotso, Chemehuevi and Mono — were collected by Kroeber in California from 1903 to 1904. For his paper "Shoshonean Dialects of California" [145], Kroeber personally collected twelve other Ute-Aztecan vocabularies bringing to nineteen the number of languages used in his classic paper. This set the framework and guidelines for subsequent linguistic research in the Great Basin. Kroeber wrote several articles regarding Numic languages. One of the more important was his "Notes on the Ute Language" [147]. He also influenced the writing and publishing of two articles on Northern Paiute (Paviotso). The first was by W. L. Marsden, an amateur linguistic of Burns, Oregon [187]; the other was by Gilbert Natches, a Paiute Indian of Lovelock, Nevada [215].

The greatest contribution to linguistics of the Great Basin was that of Edward Sapir who spent two months with a Ute linguistic informant at Whiterocks, Utah, in 1909, the year he received his doctorate from Franz Boas at Columbia. The next year, Tony Tillahash, a Southern Paiute student at Carlisle, aided Sapir as a linguistic informant. By 1918 the analysis was complete and ready for publication. The monograph finally appeared as *Southern Paiute, a Shoshonean Language* in 1931 [253]. Included are texts and translations of nineteen Southern Paiute and seven Ute myths, other texts, and a "Southern Paiute Dictionary." Wick Miller [192] wrote, of the above study, the following: "The first modern treatment of a Numic language is Sapir's now classic Southern Paiute grammar. Even though published over 40 years ago, it still ranks as one of the truly great accounts of an American Indian language."

Morris Swadesh introduced new concepts of modern linguistics to the world with his article, "Time Depths of American Linguistic Groupings" [310], using Numic and neighboring Ute-Aztecan languages in his demonstration of "glottochronology." Use of glottochronology and other new methods for solving Great

Basin linguistic problems was demonstrated by Sidney Lamb in his article, "Linguistic Prehistory in the Great Basin" [151], and in his dissertation [152]. This was followed by his publication "The Classification of the Uto-Aztecan Languages" [153].

Lamb's research depended on field work with Monos and Northern Paiutes, but the most dedicated field worker among that language group is Sven Liljeblad, who has spent months each year with native Bannocks and other Northern Paiute speakers for thirty years. Liljeblad's office in the library of the University of Nevada, Reno, is filled with boxes of word slips. The linguistic world awaits impatiently his *magnum opus* on Northern Paiute. In the meantime he is helping younger scholars like Michael J. P. Nichols, who wrote his doctoral thesis on "Northern Paiute Historical Grammar" [217]. Nichols included an acknowledgement of help and encouragement from Liljeblad, the latter of whom has published only one linguistic article on Bannock phonemes [165].

Wick Miller of the University of Utah started field work among the Shoshoni-speaking Gosiutes in 1965 following years of research and publication dealing with the Uto-Aztecan language family [193]. Through his teaching, research and writing, Shoshoni (or Central Numic) is becoming one of the best known Indian languages in America [194]. His most recent publication, *Newe Natekwinappeh: Shoshoni Stories and Dictionary* [195] can serve as an introduction to the study of Numic for college students of linguistics or as a text to help Shoshoni-speaking people keep their language. Miller's forthcoming summary of "The Numic Languages" [196] will guide the researcher to the best literature on this topic.

James Goss prepared *A Short Dictionary of the Southern Ute Language* [70] to help that tribe maintain its language. Goss has continued research and writing about Ute, having used it for his dissertation [71].

In 1975 the Southern Ute Tribal Council of Ignacio, Colorado, authorized the Ute Language Program. The tribal council and a large language committee entered into a working relationship with linguist Tom Givón to prepare dictionaries, grammars, work books, etc., which would provide the Utes the means to read and write their language. The preliminary edition of the *Ute Dictionary* [68] was printed by the Ute Press in 1979.

The theoretical problems created by the lexico-statistical dating of recent migrations of Numic speakers into the Great Basin as occurring after zero A.D., have raised problems of identification of prehistoric peoples. Nicholas A. Hopkins's article, "Great Basin Prehistory and Uto-Aztecan" [103] and the collection of papers edited by Earl H. Swanson, Jr., as *Utaztekan Prehistory* [311] are examples of concern for this problem. As in prehistory, research and publishing in linguistics is accelerating in Great Basin institutions. Catherine L. Fowler's dissertation, "Comparative Numic Ethnobiology" [55] represents modern usage of linguistics in exploration of many heretofore neglected aspects of Great Basin people's cultures.

Petroglyphs and Pictographs

Petroglyphs are designs cut into stone by chipping, rubbing, and/or cutting with another stone. Pictographs are designs painted upon stones. Both have been popular with amateur prehistorians and have been copied, photographed, sometimes removed at the cost of great labor, and often defaced. The reporting of petroglyphs and pictographs, now often combined under the term "rock art," occupies a large number of pages in all of the joint amateur-professional journals of the Great Basin such as *Southwestern Lore*, *Screening*, and *Wyoming Archaeologist*. Professional interest in Great Basin rock art, although constant over the years, is relatively less important to scholars than it is to amateurs.

Although Henry Rowe Schoolcraft devoted considerable space to rock art in his six-volume work [256], most scholarly writing on the subject starts with citations from Garrick Mallery's *Picture-Writing of the American Indians* [181]. The next work to consult is Mallery's second publication on the subject, *Pictographs of the North American Indians* [182]. Published as *Annual Reports* of the United States Bureau of Ethnology in the late nineteenth century, Mallery's lengthy discussions remain the standard reference work for North American rock art.

Surprisingly, it was the famous ethnologist of the Great Basin, Julian H. Steward, who wrote the first major professional report specifically on the regional rock art of the Great Basin. His first large scholarly work, "Petroglyphs of California and Adjoining States" [275] was issued with some of his own photographs from the Northern Paiute area of the Great Basin, Owens Valley, California. Steward included all of Nevada and Utah in his report making it a good starting point for the study of Great Basin rock art.

In her exhaustive *Great Basin Anthropology, A Bibliography*, Catherine Fowler [54] included a separate section under the heading "Petroglyphs and Pictographs." One hundred and five titles were listed. The larger works by anthropologists comparable to Steward's 1929 monograph are: *Petroglyphs of Oregon* by L. S. Cressman [32], "Indian Rock Writing in Idaho" by R. P. Erwin [50], *Prehistoric Rock Art of Nevada and Eastern California* by Robert F. Heizer and Martin A. Baumhoff [94], *Rock Art of Owens Valley, California* by Jay C. von Werlhof [341], and *Western Colorado Petroglyphs* by W. C. McKern [177].

In 1941, even though limited coverage of rock art was supplied in its published catalogue, *Indian Art of the United States* [44], the large exhibit of that title in the New York Museum of Modern Art had important repercussions. The largest and most spectacular part of the exhibit seemed almost overpowering. In the catalogue, which became a popular book, F. H. Douglas and R. d'Harnoncourt wrote, "The best preserved painted pictures are those on canyon walls in the almost rainless Southwest. Here are found immense galleries of paintings and carvings, one of which, from Barrier Canyon, Utah, has been reproduced full size for this exhibit."

Many scholars stimulated interest in Great Basin rock art for the New York exhibit. Albert B. Reagan's work in Basin art was extremely influential [242]. Steward's work was also of consequence. In his "Petroglyphs of California . . ." [275] he published four plates of photographs from eastern Utah. One showed "anthropomorphic, God-like Beings." More recently they have been featured on colored plates and black and white photographs by Campbell Grant in *Rock Art of the American Indians* [72]. The original paintings exhibited in the Museum of Modern Arts now cover the entire wall of a large exhibit room in the Utah Museum of Natural History.

Polly Schaafsma is becoming famous for her books on rock art, two of which deal with the Great Basin: *Survey report of the Rock Art of Utah* [254], and *The Rock Art of Utah: A Study from the Donald Scott Collection, Peabody Museum, Harvard University* [255]. Some other recent reports are "New Data on Rock Art Chronology in the Central Great Basin" by Thomas and Thomas [313], *Stylistic Locales and Ethnographic Groups: Petroglyphs of the Lower Snake River*, by P. E. Nesbitt [216], and *Four Great Basin Petroglyph Studies* by Robert F. Heizer, et al. [95].

For his doctoral work concerning the prehistory of western Colorado, William G. Buckles [25] devoted about one-hundred pages to the rock art of the area and its relationship to the rock art of other areas. The Utes of western Colorado revealed a consistent art tradition and indicated little influence from outside during a great length of time.

A beautifully produced and illustrated new book
on rock art comes from an unexpected author and
press, yet puts forth a most ancient theory, which is,
that petroglyphs and pictographs are true "rock writing." The book, *The Rocks Begin to Speak* by LaVan Martineau [188], is based first on Southern Paiute lore
acquired by Martineau which he learned from his
Indian foster parents. He studied published accounts
of pictographs and sign language, and traveled and
photographed extensively in the Great Basin and beyond. His chance encounter with modern cryptog-
raphy while in the U.S. Air Force in Korea led Martineau to further study and then to apply the methods
of cryptoanalysis to Indian rock art. Although the volume contains many photographs and hundreds of de-
sign elements reproduced in color, the general theory
appears no better substantiated than it was when propounded by Schoolcraft and other, even earlier, writers.

Historical Sources

Much of our knowledge of the earliest culture patterns exhibited by Great Basin Indians comes from
books usually classified as history. The diary of Escalante [19] reports on the Utes of Utah in 1776. Because more than a half century elapsed before anyone
else wrote on the subject, this diary remains an essential documentary source. Escalante was unique in his
journey into the interior of the Basin province. Few

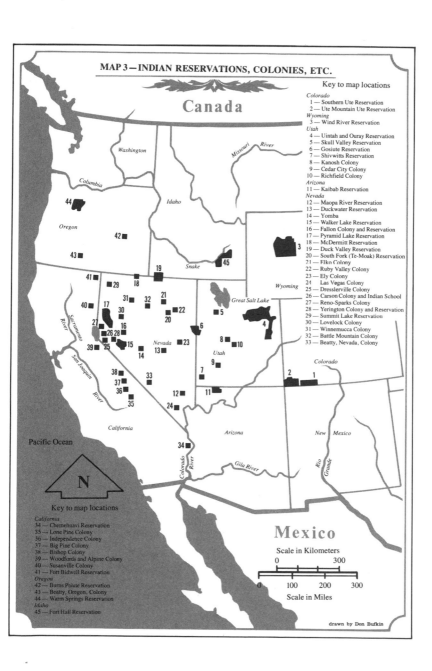

MAP 3—INDIAN RESERVATIONS, COLONIES, ETC.

Key to map locations

Colorado
1 — Southern Ute Reservation
2 — Ute Mountain Ute Reservation
Wyoming
3 — Wind River Reservation
Utah
4 — Uintah and Ouray Reservation
5 — Skull Valley Reservation
6 — Gosiute Reservation
7 — Shivwitts Reservation
8 — Kanosh Colony
9 — Cedar City Colony
10 — Richfield Colony
Arizona
11 — Kaibab Reservation
Nevada
12 — Maopa River Reservation
13 — Duckwater Reservation
14 — Yomba
15 — Walker Lake Reservation
16 — Fallon Colony and Reservation
17 — Pyramid Lake Reservation
18 — McDermitt Reservation
19 — Duck Valley Reservation
20 — South Fork (Te-Moak) Reservation
21 — Elko Colony
22 — Ruby Valley Colony
23 — Ely Colony
24 — Las Vegas Colony
25 — Dresslerville Colony
26 — Carson Colony and Indian School
27 — Reno-Sparks Colony
28 — Yerington Colony and Reservation
29 — Summit Lake Reservation
30 — Lovelock Colony
31 — Winnemucca Colony
32 — Battle Mountain Colony
33 — Beatty, Nevada, Colony

Key to map locations

California
34 — Chemehuavi Reservation
35 — Lone Pine Colony
36 — Independence Colony
37 — Big Pine Colony
38 — Bishop Colony
39 — Woodfords and Alpine Colony
40 — Susanville Colony
41 — Fort Bidwell Reservation
Oregon
42 — Burns Paiute Reservation
43 — Beatty, Oregon, Colony
44 — Warm Springs Reservation
Idaho
45 — Fort Hall Reservation

Scale in Kilometers
0   300

0   100   200   300
Scale in Miles

drawn by Don Bufkin

other Europeans penetrated the region until 1829, when Antonio Armijo traveled from Abiquiu, New Mexico to California, returning the following year along the route that became the famous Old Spanish Trail. LeRoy R. Hafen has prepared an English edition of Armijo's diary [78], essential reading on tribes of the Basin during the early nineteenth century. Other Spanish accounts touching on Great Basin Indians— especially the Utes—were utilized by Lyman Tyler in his dissertation, "Before Escalante: An Early History of the Yuta Indians and the Area North of New Mexico" [322] and in his articles, "The Spaniard and the Ute" [324] and "The Yuta Indians before 1680" [323].

Spanish-colonial contact with Basin tribes was largely confined to relations with Utes. Carling and A. A. Malouf's "The Effects of Spanish Slavery on the Indians of the Intermountain West" [185], Joseph J. Hill, "Spanish and New Mexican Exploration and Trade Northwest from New Mexico into the Great Basin" [97]; Frances L. Swadesh, *Los Primeros Pobladores* [309]; and Eleanor Lawrence, "Mexican Trade Between Santa Fe and Los Angeles, 1830–48" [159] should also be consulted by those interested in Spanish and Mexican relations with the Utes.

During the eighteenth century French-Canadians contacted the northeastern corner of the culture area. The 1742 journal of the La Vérendrye expeditionaries reports their travels southwest of the Mandan Villages, on the Missouri River in North Dakota, to a point where their Indian guides refused to travel further because they saw signs of the Snake [Shoshoni] Indians. Their journal is an important contribution to the early history of the Shoshonis. The original French report underwent translation and editing in 1927 at the able hand of Lawrence J. Burpee [158]. Burpee also contributed an article which interprets the meeting of the La Vérendrye party with the Snakes/Shoshonis in Wyoming [26]. A further contribution of this Canadian historian is his editing of the *Journal of Larocque from the Assiniboine to the Yellowstone, 1805* [157]. Larocque ascended the Missouri about a year before Lewis and Clark and gives first-contact information on many Missouri River tribes as well as Shoshonis of the Great Basin.

David Thompson, a partner in the North West Fur Company and an employee of the Hudson's Bay Company collected many valuable accounts from his Indian contacts while working in the fur trade from 1784 to 1812. One very important account, which appears to have been received by Thompson about 1800 from a Piegan (Blackfoot) mentions a war between the Shoshoni and the Piegan tribes [315]. Thompson's informant told him that in 1730 while the two tribes were up in Canada the Shoshonis had already acquired great numbers of horses, but had not obtained guns for battles with other tribes. Modern ethnographic interviews have not produced any Shoshoni legends or stories corroborating this, but it remains an important early reference to both the location of the tribes in the early eighteenth century and a yardstick for dating the diffusion of the horse.

The first American explorers to write of Great Basin Indians were members of the Lewis and Clark Expedition. Although their travels took them north of the Basin, their association with Sacajawea, the Shoshoni guide/interpreter enabled them to record names and locations of tribes of the province through interviews [16] [162] [163] [164]. Furthermore they encountered a number of Shoshonis who had traveled north into Montana and Idaho beyond their usual range. Biographies of Sacajawea often romanticize and exaggerate the true story of Indian-White relations during the expedition, but the reader interested in this important liaison for Lewis and Clark should consult the aforementioned biography by Grace Hebard [90]. Several members of the expedition published accounts of the trek but that of Patrick Gass [66] is the most important for ethnographic information about tribes of the Basin.

Lewis and Clark entered the Pacific Northwest in the wake of British fur hunting efforts. Gloria Cline presents a valuable and concise summary of exploration of the Great Basin [28] and has assembled and organized data regarding activities of the Hudson's Bay Company. Of special interest is her material about Peter Skene Ogden who was the leader of the HBC Snake River brigades from 1825 to 1830. His journals are an important source on the impact of the fur trade on some of the Basin tribes, especially those in present-day Nevada [219] [220] [221]. In addition to Ogden, readers searching for historical sources will want to consult Alexander Ross. His *The Fur Hunters of the Far West* [250] is especially important for tribes of present-day Idaho. John Work, another Hudson's Bay Company trader, left important journals for the region. *The Journal of John Work* [357], his account of the California Expeditions of 1832–1833 [358], and his "Journal . . . covering Snake Country Expeditions of 1830–31" [356] mostly concern Oregon but have several important references to Basin peoples, especially those of northeastern California.

Activities of American trappers and traders during the 1820s, 1830s, and 1840s brought them into contact with Basin tribes. The journal of Warren A. Ferris, published as *Life in the Rocky Mountains, 1830–1835* [53], Joseph A. Gebow's *Snake or Sho-Sho-Nay Vocabulary, a Guide for Trappers and Traders* [67], Osborne Russell's *Journal of a Trapper* [252], and Nathaniel Jarvis Wyeth's "Indian Tribes of the South Pass of the Rocky Mountains, The Salt Lake Basin . . ." [361] contain considerable information. Another interesting account by a trapper known as much for his mountain yarns as for accurate reporting is *The Life and Adventures of James P. Beckwourth, mountaineer, scout, and pioneer . . . written from his own dictation by T. D. Bonner* [13]. Although most of Beckwourth's major activities centered on the northern and southern Rockies, he had some experience with Great Basin tribes. If his claim of having been adopted by the Crow tribe as one of its leaders is to be believed, his account must be accepted as a comprehensive and probing description of Indian life.

Other nineteenth century accounts during the fur trade years mention Great Basin tribes attending the annual summer rendezvous held from 1825 to 1840 at various river valley sites within or at the edge of the northeastern sector of the Basin province. The journal of Captain Benjamin L. E. Bonneville provided the gifted writer, Washington Irving, a wealth of material for telling the story, *The Rocky Mountains: or Scenes, incidents, and adventures in the Far West . . .* [119]. Although Irving took literary license with Bonneville's still unpublished account, this 1837 publication gives the historian much information on location of tribes, Indian-White relations, and the impact of fur trade economics on tribes throughout the far West. One of the more vivid accounts of Indian-trapper relations was left by Zenas Leonard whose *Narrative*, printed in 1839, covers five years of activity with particular attention to Humboldt River trapping in Nevada [161]. Those readers seeking information on the activities of many well known trappers among Indians of the Basin and the Rockies will find J. Cecil Alter's *James Bridger, Trapper, Frontiersman, Scout and Guide: A Historical Narrative* [6] and many biographical sketches in LeRoy R. Hafen's ten volume *The Mountain Men and the Fur Trade of the Far West* [80] indispensable.

Most of the history of early Americans and Indians in the Great Basin remained obscure or unknown to the public until brought to light by later compilers. Much credit is due to Dale L. Morgan, whose lifetime of work with historical accounts of the West added much to Great Basin historiography. His first work, assembled and edited for the Works Projects Administration, appeared under the title, *Utah: A Guide to the State* [208]. Morgan's interests in Indians and in the fur trade dovetailed nicely and resulted in several key publications in the 1950s and 1960s. His interest in William H. Ashley, key organizer and sponsor of the Rocky Mountain trapping enterprises in the 1820s led to publication of "Diary of William Henry Ashley, March 25-June 27, 1825 . . ." [9] and the much more ambitious and complete edited volume, *The West of William H. Ashley . . . 1822–1838* [211]. Morgan had a keen eye for accuracy and detail. He sets fur trade activities in clear historical and geographic perspective. He also properly identifies the Indian tribes met by these beaver hunters. A companion volume to Morgan's *Ashley* is Harrison Clifford Dale's *The Ashley-Smith Explorations and the Discovery of a Central Route to the Pacific, 1822–1829* [34].

Although Utah and other present-day states within the Great Basin were as much a part of the history of exploration, fur trade and settlement periods of the West as other areas, few historians before Dale Morgan brought the region's rich history into proper focus. His "Utah Before the Mormons" [206], *Jedediah Smith and the Opening of the West* [202], and "Miles Goodyear and the Founding of Ogden" [203] are important in this context. For those interested in reading accounts by travelers after the California and Oregon trails were opened, Morgan's edited work, *Overland in 1846;*

Diaries and Letters of the California-Oregon Trail [210] is an extensive two-volume anthology of these narratives. Many accounts of contact with Indians of the Basin are found in these letters and diaries of "Forty-niners." *The Overland Diary of James A. Pritchard from Kentucky to California in 1849* . . . [209] was edited with Morgan's usual thoroughness and contains two maps showing routes through South Pass across the Basin in 1849 and a useful chart compiled by the editor to show all known diarists' routes through the mountains and across the desert during the California Gold Rush.

Morgan was a well-rounded scholar who contributed several works specifically on Indians, as well as several publications that should be classified as ethnogeography. His "The Administration of Indian Affairs in Utah, 1851–1858," a paper originally prepared for the United States Indian Claims Commission [201], and "Washakie and the Shoshoni: A Selection of Documents from the Records of the Utah Superintendency of Indian Affairs" [204] are essential for understanding Indian-White relations in Utah in the 1850s. *The Great Salt Lake* [200], "The Ferries of the '49'ers" [205], *The Humboldt* [199] and contributions as editorial assistant to Carl I. Wheat on the maps of Jedediah Smith [207] and in Wheat's monumental *Mapping the Transmississippi West, 1540–1861* [346] have provided proper geographical reference and analysis for understanding all aspects of Indian-White interaction during the nineteenth century Basin history.

The work of Grace Raymond Hebard has been discussed previously in connection with her biography of *Sacajawea, A Guide and Interpreter of the Lewis and Clark Expedition* [90]. Although Hebard was a fine scholar as evidenced in her work, *Washakie: An Account of Indian Resistance to the Covered Wagon and Union Pacific Railroad Invasions of Their Territory* [89], her work on perhaps the most famous American Indian woman in American history perpetrated many myths and inaccurate stories of Sacajawea. In 1907 Hebard promulgated the theory that the Shoshoni wife of Toussaint Charbonneau lived to a ripe old age, dying in present-day Wyoming in 1884. Even after several additional documentary references to the death of the wife of Charbonneau were made available, pointing to her almost certain death at Fort Manuel in 1812, Hebard continued to embrace her early view as stated most forcefully in her 1932 biography. Recently Irving W. Anderson in "Probing the Riddle of the Bird Woman" [8] has taken on Hebard and has laid the issue to rest to the satisfaction of most scholars. Unfortunately most textbooks and histories continue in promoting a larger than life portrait of "Bird Woman," Lewis and Clark's "guide."

In addition to Lewis and Clark, two other United States Government-sponsored expeditions are of special interest for Indians of the Great Basin. From 1842 to 1854 John Charles Frémont traversed several sections of the Basin and mentioned Indians by recognizable tribal names in many places. His *Report* of 1845 [62] as well as his *Memoirs* of 1887 [63] and a recent collation of his expeditions [64] are worth inspecting.

Solomon Nunes Carvalho, an artist who accompanied Frémont on his last expedition, published *Incidents of Travel and Adventure in the Far West* [27], an important supplement to Captain Frémont's own versions, the latter of which gave the Great Basin the reputation as the worst part of "the Great American Desert."

The second expeditionary, often mistakenly referred to in popular accounts as the "first" explorer of the Great Basin waterways, is John Wesley Powell. Powell's role as explorer and ethnologist/geologist are told by himself in *Exploration of the Colorado River of the West . . .* [235]; by Frederick S. Dellenbaugh, whose *A Canyon Voyage . . .* [42] provides additional information; and by Jack Hillers, a member of the 1871–1875 expedition [57]. The best modern work placing Powell in perspective is Wallace Stegner's captivating literary essay, *Beyond the Hundredth Meridian: John Wesley Powell and the Second Opening of the West* [272].

Between Frémont's last expedition and Powell's first, the Mormons began pouring into the Great Basin. Mormon-Indian relations are discussed by J. Cecil Alter, ed., "The Mormons and the Indians: New Items and Editorials from the Mormon Press" [7], Juanita Brooks, "Indian Relations on the Mormon Frontier" [23], and Lawrence G. Coates, "Mormons and Social Change among the Shoshoni, 1853–1900" [29].

Relations between Basin tribes and Anglos are analyzed in James W. Covington, "Relations between the Ute Indians and the United States Government, 1848–1900" [31]; Fowler and Fowler, "Notes on the

History of the Southern Paiutes and Western Shoshonis [56]; Omer C. Stewart, "The Western Shoshone of Nevada and the U.S. Government, 1863–1950" [305]; Stewart, "Temoke Band of Shoshone and the Oasis Concept" [306], and "Commission Findings on the Paiute Indians" by the United States Indians Claims Commission [336]. Deterioration of relations as the result of large numbers of emigrants pouring across the Basin toward the California gold fields in the 1850s may be gleaned first-hand from *Journals of Forty-Niners, Salt Lake to Los Angeles*, edited by LeRoy and Ann W. Hafen [79]. The Bannock Indian War is discussed by Brigham D. Madsen in his *The Bannock of Idaho* [179] and in an article specifically on the events which led to war in "Shoshoni-Bannock Marauders on the Oregon Trail" [180]. Army recollections of the Bannock War include General Oliver O. Howard's "Indian War Papers—Causes of the Piute and Bannock War" [107]; Chandler B. Watson, "Recollections of the Bannock War" [344]; George F. Brimlow, ed., "Two Cavalrymen's Diaries of the Bannock War, 1878" [20], W. C. Brown, "The Sheepeater Campaign, Idaho—1879" [24]; and, Stanley R. Davison, ed., "The Bannock-Piute War of 1878: Letters of Major Edwin C. Mason" [38].

The Ute War of 1854–1855 is covered by Covington [31]; Gregory C. Thompson, "Southern Ute Lands, 1848–1899: The Creation of a Reservation" [316]; and LeRoy R. Hafen, "The Fort Pueblo Massacre and the Punitive Expedition Against the Indians" [77]. Reservation history and events leading up to the second Ute-White war in 1879 are the subject of Robert Emmitt, *The Last War Trail: The Utes and the Settlement of Colorado* [49]; Marvin K. Opler, "The Ute Indian War of 1879" [224]; and, Marshall Sprague, *Massacre: The Tragedy of White River* [270]. A synopsis of reservation history and a chronology of Southern Ute history is contained in *The Southern Utes: A Tribal History* [125]. Floyd O'Neil's "The Reluctant Suzerainty: The Uintah and Ouray Reservation" [222] covers the history of the northern branch of the Utes.

Treaties for all Basin tribes are printed in Charles J. Kappler, comp., *Indian Affairs: Laws and Treaties* [135].

Special attention to historians necessitates inclusion of Carl I. Wheat, who worked for decades to assemble all known maps depicting the trans-Mississippi West, 1540–1861 [346]. Copies of maps with a discussion of each appeared in three volumes. Wheat had so many maps still on hand that he decided to continue reproducing and describing each until the total reached 1302 and extended to the year 1884, although the publication imprint retained 1861 as the terminus.

Many other historical accounts and interpretations by modern scholars on Indians of the Great Basin exist, but those listed are excellent samples of the available literature. Gloria Griffen Cline's *Exploring the Great Basin* [28] is an excellent secondary treatment and will guide the scholar to many other historical sources on expeditionaries. The aforementioned tribal histories [115] [116] [117] [118] [125] [342] are also essential reading and are important as Indian views of Indian-White relations.

Miscellaneous Publications

Physical anthropologists collaborate with archaeologists whenever skeletal material is excavated, so that their reports are usually included in the site reports. There exist some physical anthropological reports on contemporary Great Basin Indians, however, which deserve mention. The first was made by Franz Boas entitled "Anthopometry of Shoshonean Tribes" [18]. Aleš Hrdlička [109] [110] [111] included considerable data regarding Great Basin Indians in three of his publications. More recent studies have been produced by Erik K. Reed [243], James N. Spuhler [271], and K. A. R. Kennedy [141].

It is easier to know about the contemporary life of the Indians than was the case ever before because there are several monthly and weekly newspapers which specialize on reporting Great Basin Indian affairs. Two of these are tribal monthlies: *The Southern Ute Drum*, and *The Ute Bulletin*. The Indians of Nevada have supported an intertribal newspaper, *The Native Nevadan*, since 1964. Every two weeks a section of the paper reports on the affairs of about twenty of the colonies or reservations in Nevada. Since the four aboriginal linguistic groups in Nevada organized themselves into four different legal entities in order to sue the United

States government under the provisions of the Indian Claims Commission Act of 1946, those four tribal groups remain. Each has members beyond the borders of Nevada, but for each Nevada is central and dominant. Thus some items concern the Washoes as a group, or the Western Shoshonis, etc. *The Sho-Ban News* of Fort Hall is a weekly publication of the Shoshone-Bannock Tribe. All four of the papers named carry some items from the national American Indian News Association, and material is often reprinted from other local newspapers.

The Indian press covering the Great Basin today is distinct from non-Indian newspapers in that much space is devoted to athletics, Indian dancing, Pow Wows, beauty contests, and rodeos. Newspapers focus on all of the tribal and urban-Indian difficulties and express the need for good management of Indian resources. The papers report individual Indian, as well as group, accomplishments and encourage Indian self-respect, hard work and pride in Indian self-government.

In her exhaustive bibliography of Great Basin anthropology, Catherine Fowler [54] lists over a thousand titles in a special section "Federal and State Documents." Most of them are of historical importance. Another title covering all of the United States has many sections on the Great Basin summarizing the official dealings between the Indian and Federal government. A book of over 1500 pages, a *Report . . . of the Bureau of Indian Affairs* [333] was authorized by Congress in 1952. Of practical importance is another federal publication, *Federal and State Indian Reservations and Indian Trust Areas* [334] which gives location, population, land status, tribal government, tribal economy, and climate of all the modern reservations, rancherias, ranches, etc., where Great Basin Indians live and occupy restricted federal land. The group distribution is as follows: Arizona—1; California—9; Colorado—2; Idaho—1; Nevada—21; Oregon—2; Utah—4; Wyoming—1. As of 1972, there were listed roughly 16,000 Great Basin Indians.

A commercial publication which lists nearly every Indian community in the United States is Arnold Marquis' *A Guide to America's Indians: Ceremonials, Reservations, and Museums* [186]. This is useful for those wishing to visit and camp at reservations. Great Basin Indians maintain a dozen campgrounds.

The final group of important publications on Great Basin Indians consists of the *Journal of California and Great Basin Anthropology* [351] and the irregular monograph series of papers delivered at the Great Basin Anthropological conferences. The first and most important of the series is *The Current Status of Anthropological Research in the Great Basin: 1964* [40]. Seven of the authors previously mentioned in this essay presented major papers at that symposium. For example, Malouf wrote on "Ethnohistory of the Great Basin," Downs on environment and cultural development, Don D. Fowler on "Great Basin Social Organization," Wick Miller on "Anthropological Linguistics in the Great Basin,"

Stewart on "Tribal Distributions and Boundaries in the Great Basin." Stewart's article included thirty maps showing some bases for the aboriginal areas of the Great Basin Indians. These were used in cases before the U.S. Indian Claims Commission. The final areas claimed and the areas accepted by the Indian Claims Commission were also outlined.

Four other monographs have been produced from Great Basin Anthropological Conference papers. Two had more restricted themes: *Native American Politics: Power Relations in the Western Great Basin Today*, edited by Ruth M. Houghton [106]; and *Great Basin Cultural Ecology: A Symposium*, edited by Don D. Fowler [58]. *Politics* attracted papers by eight authors and *Ecology* contained fifteen papers. Two other monographs were *Great Basin Anthropological Conference 1970: Selected Papers*, edited by C. Melvin Aikens [4] and *Selected Papers from the 14th Great Basin Anthropology Conference* [321]. Variations in format result from having different editors, and a number of different publishers.

A final comment is necessary for discussion of the Great Basin volume in the Smithsonian Institution's *Handbook of North American Indians*, in preparation under the general editorship of William C. Sturtevant. Like the others in the twenty-volume series, the Great Basin volume, edited by Warren d'Azevedo [41], has been in preparation since 1971. Roughly two-thirds of the forty-one articles were completed by 1978. General topics to be covered are "History of Research", "Natural and Cultural Environment," "Linguistics," "Prehistory" (with twelve articles), "History," "Religious Movements," nine ethnographies, and several "Special Topics" including mythology, music and rock art. These essays provide interpretive overviews and are intended to guide the reader to select listings of other works on specific topics. The final volume in the series is designed as a general index. Readers seeking a short encyclopedic summary on a specific aspect of Great Basin culture and history should consult the original *Handbook* [100], completed in 1910 under the editorship of Frederick Webb Hodge.

ALPHABETICAL LIST AND INDEX

* denotes items suitable for secondary school students

Item
No.

Essay
Page
No.

[1] Aberle, David F., and Omer C. Stewart. 1957. *Navaho and Ute Peyotism: A Chronological and Distributional Study.* University of Colorado Series in Anthropology 6. Boulder: University of Colorado. (21)

[2] Adovasio, J. M. 1974. "Prehistoric North American Basketry," in *Collected Papers on Aboriginal Basketry*, pp. 98–148. Nevada State Museum Anthropological Papers 16. (46)

[3] Aikens, C. Melvin. 1970. *Hogup Cave.* University of Utah Anthropological Papers 93. (3, 13)

[4] ———, ed. 1971. *Great Basin Anthropological Conference 1970 — Selected Papers.* University of Oregon Anthropological Papers 1. (70)

[5] ———. 1978. "The Far West," in *Ancient Native Americans*, ed. Jesse D. Jennings, pp. 131–81. San Francisco: W. H. Freeman.   (13)

*[6] Alter, J. Cecil. 1925. *James Bridger, Trapper, Frontiersman, Scout and Guide: A Historical Narrative.* Salt Lake City: Shepard Book Company; Columbus, Ohio: Long's College Book Shop. New rev. ed., Norman: University of Oklahoma Press, 1962.   (60)

[7] ———, ed. 1944. "The Mormons and the Indians: News Items and Editorials from the Mormon Press." *Utah Historical Quarterly* 12:49–68.   (64)

[8] Anderson, Irving W. 1973. "Probing the Riddle of the Bird Woman." *Montana, the Magazine of Western History* 23 (October):2–17.   (63)

[9] Ashley, William Henry [1825] 1954. "Diary of William Henry Ashley, March 25-June 27, 1825," ed. Dale L. Morgan. *Missouri Historical Society Bulletin.* 11:9–40, 158–86, 279–302. Also see [211].   (61)

*[10]   Bailey, Paul. 1954. *Walkara, Hawk of the Mountains*. Los Angeles: Westernlore Press.   (ix)

*[11]   ———. 1957. *Wovoka: The Indian Messiah*. Los Angeles: Westernlore Press.   (36)

[12]   Barrett, S. A. 1917. "The Washo Indians." *Publications of the Public Museum of the City of Milwaukee* 2(1):1–52. Reprinted as *The Washo Indians*, New York: AMS, 1978.   (45)

[13]   [Beckwourth, James P.] 1856. *The life and adventures of James P. Beckwourth, mountaineer, scout, and pioneer, and chief of the Crow nation of Indians, written from his own dictation by T. D. Bonner*. London: S. Low, Son and Company. New ed., ed. with preface by Charles G. Leland, London: T. F. Unwin, 1892. Reprint in facsimile of 1856 ed., New York: Knopf, 1931. New ed., with intro. and notes by Delmont R. Oswald, Lincoln: University of Nebraska Press, 1972.   (59)

[14]   Bedwell, Stephen F. 1973. *Fort Rock Basin: Prehistory and Environment*. Eugene: University of Oregon Press.   (3)

[15] Bettinger, Robert L. 1979. "Multivariate Statistical Analysis of Regional Subsistence — Settlement Model for Owens Valley." *American Antiquity* 44(3):455–70. (42)

[16] Biddle, Nicholas. 1814. *History of the Expedition under the Command of Captains Lewis and Clark, to the sources of the Missouri, thence across the Rocky Mountains and down the River Columbia to the Pacific Ocean. Performed during the years 1804–5–6. By order of the government of the United States. Prepared for the press by Paul Allen, esquire.* . . . 2 vols. Philadelphia: Bradford and Inskeep; New York: Abm. H. Inskeep, J. Maxwell, printer. New ed., New York: Allerton Book Company, 1922. Reprinted, New York: AMS, 1973. (58)

[17] Bliss, W. L. 1950. "Birdshead Cave, a Stratified Site in the Wind River Basin, Wyoming." *American Antiquity* 15:187–96. (13)

[18] Boas, Franz. 1899. "Anthropometry of Shoshonean Tribes." *American Anthropologist*, n. s. 1:751–58. (67)

[19] Bolton, Herbert Eugene. 1951. *Pageant in the Wilderness; The Story of the Escalante Expedition to the Interior Basin, 1776, including the Diary and Itinerary of Father Escalante, translated and annotated by Herbert E. Bolton.* Salt Lake City: Utah State Historical Society. (17, 19, 27, 54)

[20] Brimlow, George F., ed. 1967. "Two Cavalrymen's Diaries of the Bannock War, 1878." *Oregon Historical Quarterly* 68:221–58, 293–316. (65)

[21] Brink, Pamela J. 1969. "The Pyramid Lake Paiute of Nevada." Ph.D. dissertation, Boston University. Ann Arbor: University Microfilms. (43)

[22] ———. 1971. "Paviotso Child Training: Notes." *Indian Historian* 4(1):47–50, 66. (43)

[23] Brooks, Juanita. 1944. "Indian Relations on the Mormon Frontier." *Utah Historical Quarterly* 12:1–48. (64)

[24] Brown, W. C. 1925–1926. "The Sheepeater Campaign, Idaho-1879." *Tenth Biennial Report of The State Historical Society of Idaho* 10:27–51. Reprinted, Boise: Syms-York, 1926. (65)

[25] Buckles, William G. 1971. "The Uncompahgre Complex: Historic Ute Archaeology and Prehistoric Archaeology on the Uncompahgre Plateau in West Central Colorado." Ph.D. dissertation, University of Colorado. Ann Arbor: University Microfilms. (53)

[26] Burpee, Lawrence J. 1945. "La Vérendrye—Pathfinder of the West." *Annals of Wyoming* 17:107–11. (57)

[27] Carvalho, Solomon Nunes. 1856. *Incidents of Travel and Adventure in the Far West; with Col. Fremont's Last Expedition across the Rocky Mountains; including three months' residence in Utah, and a perilous trip across the Great American Desert to the Pacific.* New York: Derby and Jackson. Reissued, Cincinnati: H. W. Derby and Company, 1857. Reprint of 1857 cd., New York: Arno, 1973. (64)

*[28] Cline, Gloria Griffen. 1963. *Exploring the Great Basin.* Norman: University of Oklahoma Press. (58, 66)

[29] Coates, Lawrence G. 1972. "Mormons and Social Change among the

Shoshoni, 1853–1900." *Idaho Yesterdays* 15 (Winter):3–11.   (64)

[30] Collins, Thomas W. 1971. "The Northern Ute Economic Development Program: Social and Cultural Dimensions." Ph.D. dissertation, University of Colorado. Ann Arbor: University Microfilms.   (23)

[31] Covington, James W. 1949. "Federal Relations Between Ute Indians and the United States Government, 1848–1900." Ph.D. dissertation, University of Oklahoma.   (64, 65)

[32] Cressman, L. S. 1937. *Petroglyphs of Oregon.* Eugene: University of Oregon Press.   (52)

*[33] Curtis, Edward Sheriff. 1926. *Northern Paiute, Washo, and Others.* Vol. 15 of *The North American Indians: Being a Series of Volumes Picturing and Describing the Indians of the United States and Alaska*, ed. Frederick Webb Hodge. 20 vols. Cambridge: Harvard University Press. Reprinted, New York: Johnson, 1970.   (39, 45)

[34] Dale, Harrison Clifford. 1918. *The Ashley-Smith Explorations and the Discovery*

of a Central Route to the Pacific, 1822–1829. Cleveland: The Arthur H. Clark Company. Rev. ed., 1941. (61)

[35] Dangberg, Grace. 1957. "Letters to Jack Wilson the Paiute Prophet." *Bureau of American Ethnology Bulletin* 164:279–96. Washington: Government Printing Office. (36)

[36] ———. 1968. *Washo Tales.* Occasional Paper of the Nevada State Museum. Carson City, Nevada. (45)

[37] Davis, E. L., and R. Shutler, Jr. 1969. "Recent Discoveries of Fluted Points in California and Nevada." *Anthropological Papers of the Nevada State Museum* 14:154–77. (6)

[38] Davison, Stanley R., ed. 1972. "The Bannock-Piute War of 1878: Letters of Major Edwin C. Mason." *Journal of the West* 11:128–42. (65)

[39] d'Azevedo, Warren L., ed. 1963. *The Washo Indians of California and Nevada.* University of Utah Anthropological Papers 67. (46)

[40] d'Azevedo, Warren L., Wilbur A. Davis, Don D. Fowler, and Wayne Suttles, eds. 1966. *The Current Status of Anthropological Research in the Great Basin: 1964.* Reno: Desert Research Institute of the University of Nevada.   (69)

[41] d'Azevedo, Warren L., ed. (in press). *Great Basin.* Vol. 11 of *Handbook of North American Indians*, gen. ed. William C. Sturtevant. 20 vols. Washington: Government Printing Office for the Smithsonian Institution.   (70)

[42] Dellenbaugh, Frederick Samuel. 1908. *A Canyon Voyage; the Narrative of the Second Powell Expedition down the Green-Colorado River from Wyoming, and the Explorations on Land, in the years 1871 and 1872, by Frederick S. Dellenbaugh, artist and assistant topographer of the expedition.* New York: G. P. Putnam's Sons. 2d ed., New Haven: Yale University Press, 1926. Reprinted, 1962.   (64)

[43] Densmore, Frances. 1922. *Northern Ute Music.* Bureau of American Ethnology Bulletin 75. Washington: Government Printing Office.   (22)

*[44] Douglas, F. H., and R. D'Harnoncourt. 1941. *Indian Art of the United States*. New York: The Museum of Modern Art. (52)

[45] Downs, James F. 1961. "Washo Religion." University of California Anthropological Records 16(9):365–85. (46)

*[46] ———. 1966. *The Two Worlds of the Washo, an Indian Tribe of California and Nevada*. New York: Holt, Rinehart and Winston. (46)

[47] Du Bois, Cora. 1939. *The 1870 Ghost Dance*. University of California Anthropological Records 3:1–151. (37)

[48] Duffield, M. S. 1904. "Aboriginal Remains in Nevada and Utah." *American Anthropologist*, n. s. 6:148–50. (9)

[49] Emmitt, Robert. 1954. *The Last War Trail: The Utes and the Settlement of Colorado*. Norman: University of Oklahoma Press. Reprinted, 1972. (66)

[50] Erwin, R. P. 1930. "Indian Rock Writing in Idaho." *Biennial Report of the State Historical Society of Idaho* 12:35–113. (52)

[51]   Euler, Robert C. 1966. *Southern Paiute
       Ethnohistory*. University of Utah An-
       thropological Papers 78.   (26)

*[52]   ———. 1972. *The Paiute People*. Phoe-
       nix: Indian Tribal Series.   (26)

[53]   Ferris, Warren Angus. 1940. *Life in the
       Rocky Mountains: A Diary of Wanderings
       on the Sources of the Rivers Missouri, Co-
       lumbia, and Colorado from February, 1830,
       to November, 1835*, ed. Paul C. Phillips.
       Denver: The Old West Publishing
       Company.   (28, 59)

[54]   Fowler, Catherine S. 1969. *Great Basin
       Anthropology, A Bibliography*. Desert Re-
       search Institute, Social Sciences and
       Humanities Publication No. 5. Reno:
       Desert Research Institute of the Uni-
       versity of Nevada.   (viii, 52, 68)

[55]   ———. 1972. "Comparative Numic
       Ethnobiology." Ph.D. dissertation, Uni-
       versity of Pittsburgh. Ann Arbor: Uni-
       versity Microfilms.   (50)

[56]   Fowler, Catherine S., and Don D.
       Fowler. 1971. "Notes on the History of
       the Southern Paiutes and Western

Shoshonis." *Utah Historical Quarterly* 39:95–113. (65)

[57] Fowler, Don. D., ed. 1971. *"Photographed all the best scenery": Jack Hiller's Diary of the Powell Expedition, 1871–1875.* Salt Lake City: University of Utah Press. (26, 64)

[58] ———, ed. 1972. *Great Basin Cultural Ecology: A Symposium.* Desert Research Institute Publications in the Social Sciences No. 8. Reno: Desert Research Institute of the University of Nevada. (70)

[59] Fowler, Don D., and Catherine S. Fowler, eds. 1970. "Stephen Powers' 'The Life and Culture of the Washo and Paiutes.'" *Ethnohistory* 17:117–49. See [237]. (38)

[60] ———, eds. 1971. *Anthropology of the Numa: John Wesley Powell's Manuscripts on the Numic Peoples of Western North America, 1868–1880.* Smithsonian Contributions to Anthropology No. 14. (18, 25, 47)

[61] Freed, Stanley A. 1960. "Changing Washo Kinship." *University of California Anthropological Records* 14(6):349–418. (46)

[62]   Frémont, John Charles. 1845. *Report of the Exploring Expedition to the Rocky Mountains in the year 1842, and to Oregon and North California in the years 1843–'44.* 28th Cong., 2d sess. Senate Ex. Doc. 174. Washington: Gales and Seaton, printers. Reprinted in *Narratives of Exploration and Adventure*, ed. Alan Nevins, New York: Longmans, Green, 1956.   (63)

[63]   ———. 1887. *Memoirs of My Life.* Chicago and New York: Belford, Clarke and Company.   (63)

[64]   ———. 1970–73. *The Expeditions of John Charles Frémont*, ed. Donald Jackson and Mary Lee Spence. 2 vols. Urbana: University of Illinois Press.   (63)

[65]   Frison, George C. 1978. *Prehistoric Hunters of the High Plains.* New York: Academic Press.   (1)

*[66]   Gass, Patrick. 1807. *A Journal of the Voyages and Travels of a Corps of Discovery under the Command of Capt. Lewis and Capt. Clark of the Army of the United States, from the Mouth of the River Missouri through the Interior parts of North*

America to the Pacific Ocean, during the years 1804, 1805 and 1806. . . . Pittsburgh: Printed by Zadok Cramer for David McKeehan. New ed., Philadelphia: for M. Carey, 1810. Reprinted, Minneapolis: Ross and Haines, 1958. (58)

[67] Gebow, Joseph A. 1864. *Snake or Sho-Sho-Nay Vocabulary, A Guide for Trappers and Traders.* Camp Douglas: Printed at the "Dailey Union Vedette" Book and Job Office. (47, 59)

[68] Givón, Tom. 1979. *Ute Dictionary, Preliminary Edition. NUU — ?APÁĜA — PIPQ?Ó — QWA — TI* Ignacio, Colorado: The Southern Ute Tribe. (50)

[69] Gomberg, William, and Joy Leland. 1963. *We Need to be Shown: A Study of the Talents, Work and Potential and Aspirations of the Pyramid Lake Paiute.* Washington: Bureau of Indian Affairs. (43)

[70] Goss, James S. 1961. *A Short Dictionary of the Southern Ute Language.* Ignacio, Colorado: Southern Ute Tribe. (50)

[71]   ———. 1972. "Ute Lexical and Pho-
nological Patterns." Ph.D. dissertation,
University of Chicago.   (50)

*[72]   Grant, Campbell. 1967. *Rock Art of the
American Indians.* New York: T. Y.
Crowell.   (53)

[73]   Graves, Theodore D. 1961. "Time Perspective and the Deferred Gratification
Pattern in a Tri-Ethnic Community."
Ph.D. dissertation, University of Pennsylvania. Ann Arbor: University Microfilms.   (25)

[74]   Grosscup, G. L. 1960. *The Culture History of Lovelock Cave, Nevada.* University
of California Archaeological Survey
Reports No. 52.   (7)

[75]   Gruhn, R. 1961. *The Archaeology of Wilson Butte Cave, South-Central Idaho.* Occasional Papers of the Idaho State University Museum No. 6.   (3)

[76]   Gunnerson, J. H. 1956. "A Fluted Point
Site in Utah." *American Antiquity*
21:412–14.   (3)

[77]   Hafen, LeRoy R. 1927. "The Fort
Pueblo Massacre and the Punitive Ex-

pedition Against the Indians." *Colorado Magazine* 4:49–58. (65)

[78] ———. 1954. *Old Spanish Trail; Santa Fe to Los Angeles; with extracts from contemporary records and including diaries of Antonio Armijo and Orville Pratt.* Glendale, California: The Arthur H. Clark Company. (56)

[79] ———, ed. 1954. *Journals of Forty-niners, Salt Lake to Los Angeles.* Glendale, Calif.: Arthur H. Clark Company. (65)

[80] ———, ed. 1965–1972. *The Mountain Men and the Fur Trade of the Far West.* 10 vols. Glendale, Calif.: The Arthur H. Clark Company. See vol. 10, "Bibliography and Index." (60)

[81] Haines, Frances. 1938. "The Northward Spread of Horses among Plains Indians." *American Anthropologist,* n. s. 40:429–36. (19)

[82] ———. 1966. "Horses for Western Indians." *American West* 3:4–15. (19)

[83] Harner, Nellie Shaw. 1974. *Indians of Coo-yu-ee Pah (Pyramid Lake).* Sparks,

Nevada: Davis Printing and Publishing
Company.   (ix)

[84] Harrington, M. R. 1948. *An Ancient Site
at Borax Lake, California.* Southwest
Museum Papers No. 16. Los Angeles:
The Southwest Museum.   (1)

[85] Harrington, M. R., and R. D. Simpson.
1961. *Tule Springs, Nevada, with Other
Evidences of Pleistocene Man in North
America.* Southwest Museum Papers No.
18. Los Angeles: The Southwest
Museum.   (3)

[86] Harris, Jack Sargent. 1940. "The White
Knife Shoshone of Nevada," In *Accultu-
ration in Seven American Indian Tribes*, ed.
Ralph Linton, pp. 39–116. New York:
D. Appleton-Century Company. See
[167].   (33)

*[87] Haynes, C. Vance, Jr. 1969. "The Ear-
liest Americans." *Science* 166:709–15.   (x)

[88] ———. 1973. "The Calico Site: Artifacts or Geofacts?" *Science* 181:305–10.   (4)

*[89] Hebard, Grace R. 1930. *Washakie: An
Account of Indian Resistance to the Covered*

Wagon and Union Pacific Railroad Invasions of Their Territory. Cleveland: The Arthur H. Clark Company. Reprinted, New York: AMS, 1980. (63)

*[90] ————. 1932. *Sacajawea, Guide and Interpreter of the Lewis and Clark Expedition, with an Account of the Travels of Toussaint Charbonneau, and of Jean Baptiste, the Expedition Papoose.* Glendale, California: The Arthur H. Clark Company. Reprinted, 1957. (28, 58, 63)

[91] Heizer, Robert F. 1958. *Current Views on Great Basin Archaeology.* University of California Archaeological Survey Reports No. 42. (7)

[92] ————. 1970. "Ethnographic Notes on the Northern Paiute of the Humboldt Sink, West-Central Nevada," in *Languages and Cultures of Western North America*, ed. Earl H. Swanson, Jr. See [312]. (42)

[93] Heizer, Robert F., and A. D. Krieger. 1956. *The Archaeology of Humboldt Cave, Churchill County, Nevada.* University of California Publications in American Archaeology and Ethnology 47. (7)

[94]   Heizer, Robert F., and Martin A.
        Baumhoff. 1962. *Prehistoric Rock Art of
        Nevada and Eastern California.* Berkeley:
        University of California Press.   (52)

[95]   Heizer, Robert F., et al. 1974. *Four
        Great Basin Petroglyph Studies.* University
        of California Archaeological Research
        Facility Contributions No. 20.   (53)

[96]   Hester, Thomas R. 1973. *Chronological
        Ordering of Great Basin Prehistory.* Uni-
        versity of California Archaeological Re-
        search Facility Contributions No. 17.   (8)

[97]   Hill, Joseph J. 1930. "Spanish and New
        Mexican Exploration and Trade into
        the Great Basin." *Utah Historical Quar-
        terly* 3:2–23.   (56)

[98]   Hittman, Michael. 1973. "The 1870
        Ghost Dance of the Walker River Res-
        ervation: A Reconstruction." *Ethnohis-
        tory* 20:247–78.   (37)

[99]   ———. 1973. "Ghost Dances, Disillu-
        sionment and Opiate Addiction: An
        Ethnohistory of Smith and Mason Val-
        ley Paiutes." Ph.D. dissertation, Uni-
        versity of New Mexico. Ann Arbor:
        University Microfilms.   (37)

*[100] Hodge, Frederick Webb, ed. 1907, 1910. *Handbook of American Indians North of Mexico.* 2 vols. United States Bureau of American Ethnology Bulletin 30. Washington: Government Printing Office. Reprinted, New York: Pageant Books, 1959; Totowa, N.J.: Rowman and Littlefield, 1975. (71)

[101] Hoebel, E. Adamson. 1935. "The Sun Dance of the Ilekandika Shoshone." *American Anthropologist,* n.s. 37:570–81. (33)

*[102] Hopkins, Sarah Winnemucca. 1883. *Life Among the Piutes; Their Wrongs and Claims,* ed. Horace Mann. Boston: Cuppies, Upham and Company; New York: George P. Putnam's Sons. Reprinted, Bishop, California: Chalfant Press. 1969. (36, 47)

[103] Hopkins, Nicholas A. 1965. "Great Basin Prehistory and Uto-Aztecans." *American Antiquity* 31:48–60. (50)

[104] Houghton, Ruth M. 1969. "The Fort McDermitt Indian Reservation: Social Structure and the Distribution of Political and Economic Power." Master's thesis, University of Oregon. (44)

[105]   ———. 1973. "Adaptive Strategies in an American Indian Reservation Community: The War on Poverty, 1965–1971." Ph.D. dissertation, University of Oregon. Ann Arbor: University Microfilms.   (44)

[106]   Houghton, Ruth M., ed. 1973. *Native American Politics: Power Relationships in the Western Great Basin Today.* Reno: Bureau of Governmental Research, University of Nevada.   (70)

[107]   Howard, Oliver O. 1887. "Indian War Papers—Causes of the Piute and Bannock War." "Outbreak of the Bannock War." *Overland Monthly* 9 (May):492–98, (June):587:92.   (65)

[108]   Hoyt, Milton. 1967. "Development of Education among the Southern Utes." Ed.D. dissertation, University of Colorado. Ann Arbor: University Microfilms.   (25)

[109]   Hrdlička, Aleš. 1906. "Contributions to the Physical Anthropology of California, based on Collections in the Department of Anthropology of the University of California and in the U.S.

National Museum." *University of California Publications in American Archaeology and Ethnology* 4(2):49–64. (67)

[110] ———. 1908. *Physiological and Medical Observations among the Indians of the Southwestern United States and Northern Mexico.* Bureau of American Ethnology Bulletin 34. Washington: Government Printing Office. (67)

[111] ———. 1909. "On the Stature of the Indians of the Southwest and of Northern Mexico," in *Anthropological Essays Presented to Frederick Ward Putnam in Honor of his Seventieth Birthday, April 16, 1909. . . .* New York: G. E. Stechert and Company. (67)

[112] Hultkrantz, Åke. 1955. "The Origin of Death Myth as Found among the Wind River Shoshoni Indians." *Ethnos* 20:127–36. (32)

[113] ———. 1956. "Configurations of Religious Belief among the Wind River Shoshoni." *Ethos* 21:194–215. (32)

[114] ———. 1961. "The Shoshone in the Rocky Mountain Area." *The Annals of*

Wyoming 33(1):19–41. [Translated from Swedish as it appeared in *YMER* 3(1956):167–87].   (32)

*[115] Intertribal Council of Nevada. 1976. *NEWW: A Western Shoshone History.* Reno: Intertribal Council of Nevada. (35, 66)

*[116] ———. 1976. *NUMA: A Northern Paiute History.* Reno: Intertribal Council of Nevada.   (44, 66)

*[117] ———. 1976. *NUWUVI: A Southern Paiute History.* Reno: Intertribal Council of Nevada.   (26, 66)

*[118] ———. 1976. *WA SHE SHU: A Washo Tribal History.* Reno: Intertribal Council of Nevada.   (46, 66)

*[119] Irving, Washington. 1837. *The Rocky Mountains: or, Scenes, Incidents, and Adventures in the Far West; digested from the Journal of Captain B. L. E. Bonneville, of the Army of the United States, and illustrated from various other sources.* Philadelphia: Carey, Lea and Blanchard. Rev. ed., *The Adventures of Captain Bonneville, U. S. A., in the Rocky Mountains and the Far West.* . . . , New York: G. P. Put-

nam's Sons, 1868. New ed., ed. with an intro. by Edgeley W. Todd, Norman: University of Oklahoma Press, 1961.　(60)

[120]　Irwin, Henry T. 1968. "The Itama: Late Pleistocene Inhabitants of the Plains of the United States and Canada and the American Southwest." Ph.D. dissertation, Harvard University.　(2)

[121]　———. 1971. "Developments in Early Man Studies in Western North America." *Arctic Anthropology* 8(2):42– 67.　(2)

[122]　Irwin-Williams, Cynthia, H. Irwin, and George Agogino. 1962. "Ice Age Man versus Mammoth in Wyoming." *National Geographic Magazine* 121(6):828– 37.　(2)

[123]　Irwin-Williams, Cynthia, H. Irwin, George Agogino, and C. Vance Haynes, Jr. 1973. "Hell Gap: Paleo-Indian Occupation on the High Plains." *Plains Anthropologist* 19:40– 53.　(2)

[124]　Jacobsen, William H., Jr. 1965. "A Grammar of the Washo Language." Ph.D. dissertation, University of

California, Berkeley. Ann Arbor: University Microfilms. (46)

*[125] Jefferson, James, Robert W. Delaney, and C. Gregory Thompson. 1972. *The Southern Utes: A Tribal History.* Ignacio, Colorado: The Southern Ute Tribe. (22, 24, 66)

[126] Jennings, Jesse D. 1957. *Danger Cave.* Society for American Archaeology Memoir 14; University of Utah Anthropological Papers 27. Reprinted, Salt Lake City: University of Utah Press, 1970. (3, 12)

[127] ———. 1965. "Prehistory," in *The Native Americans: Prehistory and Ethnology of the North American Indians*, ed. R. F. Spencer and Jesse D. Jennings, pp. 9–57. New York: Harper and Row. 2d, revised ed. issued as *The Native Americans: Ethnology and Backgrounds of the North American Indians*, 1977. See Chapter 1, "Perspective," pp. 2–22; 5, "Western North America—Plateau, Basin, California," pp. 164–250. (14)

*[128] ———. 1968. *Prehistory of North America.* New York: McGraw-Hill. New ed., 1974. (14)

[129] Jennings, Jesse D., and E. Norbeck. 1955. "Great Basin Prehistory: A Review." *American Antiquity* 21:1–11. (13)

[130] Jennings, Jesse D., ed. 1978. *Ancient Native Americans.* San Francisco: W. H. Freeman. Also see [5]. (14)

[131] Jessor, Richard, Theodore D. Graves, Robert C. Hanson, and Shirley L. Jessor. 1968. *Society, Personality and Deviant Behavior.* New York: Holt, Rinehart and Winston. (25)

[132] Johnson, Charles Clark. 1963. "A Study of Modern Southwestern Indian Leadership." Ph.D. dissertation, University of Colorado. Ann Arbor: University Microfilms. (25)

[133] Jones, J. A. 1955. *The Sun Dance of the Northern Ute.* Bureau of American Ethnology Bulletin 157. Washington: Government Printing Office. (22)

[134] Jorgensen, Joseph G. 1972. *The Sun Dance Religion: Power for the Powerless.* Chicago: University of Chicago Press. Reprinted. (22, 23)

[135]   Kappler, Charles J., comp. 1903–41.
        Indian Affairs: Laws and Treaties. 5 vols.
        Washington, D.C.: Government Print-
        ing Office. Vol. 2, *Treaties,* 1904. Senate
        Doc. no. 319, 59th Cong. 2d sess., serial
        no. 4624. Reprinted, New York: Inter-
        land 1972.   (66)

[136]   Kelly, Isabel T. 1932. "Ethnography of
        the Surprise Valley Paiute." *University of
        California Publications in American Ar-
        chaeology and Ethnology* 31(3):67–210.   (25,
                                                   40, 41)

[137]   ———. 1934. "Southern Paiute Bands."
        American Anthropologist, n. s. 36:548–60.   (25)

[138]   ———. 1936. "Chemehuevi Shaman-
        ism," in *Essays in Anthropology Presented
        to A. L. Kroeber,* ed. Robert H. Lowie,
        pp. 129–42. Berkeley: University of
        California Press.   (25)

[139]   ———. 1939. "Southern Paiute Sha-
        manism." *University of California An-
        thropological Records* 2:151–67.   (25)

[140]   ———. 1964. *Southern Paiute Ethnog-
        raphy.* University of Utah Anthropolog-
        ical Papers No. 69.   (25)

[141] Kennedy, K. A. R. 1959. *The Aboriginal Population of the Great Basin.* University of California Archaeological Survey Report 45. (67)

[142] Knack, Martha Carol. 1975 "Contemporary Southern Paiute Household Structure and Bilateral Kinship Clusters." Ph.D. dissertation, University of Michigan. Ann Arbor: University Microfilms. Reissued as *Life is with People.* Socorro, N.M.: Ballena Press, 1980. (26)

[143] ———. 1977. "A Short Resource History of Pyramid Lake, Nevada." *Ethnohistory* 24(1):47–63. (44)

[144] Knack, Martha C., and Omer C. Stewart. (in press). *As Long as the Rivers Shall Run: Economic Ethnohistory of the Pyramid Lake Indian Reservation.* (44)

[145] Kroeber, Alfred Louis. 1907. "Shoshonean Dialects of California." *University of California Publications in American Archaeology and Ethnology* 4:66–164. (47)

[146] ———. 1907. "The Washo Language of East-Central California and Nevada."

University of California Publications in American Archaeology and Ethnology 4:251–317.   (45)

[147]   ———. 1908. "Notes on the Ute Language." *American Anthropologist,* n. s. 10:74–87.   (17, 48)

[148]   ———. 1925. *Handbook of the Indians of California.* Bureau of American Ethnology Bulletin 78. Reprinted, Berkeley: California Book Company, 1953; St. Clair Shores, Mich.: Scholarly Press, 1972.   (25, 45)

[149]   ———. 1957. "Coefficients of Cultural Similarity of Northern Paiute Bands; Ethnographic Interpretations." *University of California Publications in American Archaeology and Ethnology* 47:209–14.   (44)

[150]   Laird, Carobeth. 1977. *The Chemehuevi.* Banning, Calif.: Malki Museum Press.   (26)

[151]   Lamb, Sidney M. 1958. "Linguistic Prehistory in the Great Basin." *International Journal of American Linguistics* 24:95–100.   (49)

[152]   ———. 1958. "Mono Grammar." Ph.D.

dissertation, University of California, Berkeley.   (49)

[153] ———. 1964. "The Classification of the Uto-Aztecan Languages." *University of California Publications in Linguistics* 34:106–25.   (49)

[154] Lang, Gottfried O. 1953. *A Study in Culture Contact and Culture Change: The Whiterocks Utes in Transition.* University of Utah Anthropological Papers 15.   (22)

[155] ———. 1954. "The Ute Development Program: A Study in Culture Change in an Underdeveloped Area Within the United States." Ph.D. dissertation, Cornell University. Ann Arbor: University Microfilms.   (23)

[156] Langer, Thomas S. 1954." Normative Behavior and Emotional Adjustment in a Tri-ethnic Community." Ph.D. dissertation, Columbia University.   (24)

[157] Larocque, Francois Antoine [1805] 1910. *Journal of Larocque from the Assiniboine to the Yellowstone, 1805,* ed. with notes by Lawrence J. Burpee. Ottawa: Government Printing Bureau.   (57)

[158]   La Vérendrye, Pierre Gautier de Varennes, sieur de. [1738–1749] 1927.
*Journals and Letters of Pierre Gautier de
Varennes de La Vérendrye and his Sons,
with Correspondence between the Governors
of Canada and the French Court, touching
the Search for the Western Sea*, ed. with intro. and notes by Lawrence J. Burpee.
Toronto: The Champlain Society.   (57)

[159]   Lawrence, Eleanor. 1931. "Mexican
Trade Between Santa Fe and Los
Angeles, 1830–48." *California Historical
Quarterly* 10:27–39.   (56)

[160]   Leakey, Louis S. B., Ruth D. Simpson,
and Thomas Clements. 1968. "Archaeological Excavations in the Calico
Mountains, California: Preliminary Report." *Science* 160:1022–23.   (4)

*[161]   Leonard, Zenas. 1839. *Narrative of the
Adventures of Zenas Leonard, a Native of
Clearfield County, Pa. who spent Five years
in the Trapping for Furs, Trading with the
Indians, &c., &c., of the Rocky Mountains.*
Clearfield, Pa.: Printed and published
by D. W. Moore. New ed., ed. W. F.
Wagner, Cleveland: The Burrows
Brothers Company, 1904. Reissued, ed.

Milo Milton Quaife, Chicago: The
Lakeside Press, 1934; New ed., printed
as *Adventures of Zenas Leonard, Fur
Trader*, ed. John C. Ewers, Norman:
University of Oklahoma Press, 1959.　　(60)

[162] Lewis, Meriwether. 1806. *Message from
the President of the United States, com-
municating discoveries made in exploring
the Missouri, Red River and Washita, by
Captains Lewis and Clark.* . . . City of
Washington: A. & G. Way, printers.　　(58)

[163] Lewis, Meriwether, and John Ordway.
[1803–1806] 1916. *The Journals of Captain Meriwether Lewis and Sergeant John
Ordway, kept on the Expedition of Western
Exploration, 1803–1806*, ed. with intro.
and notes by Milo M. Quaife. Madison:
Historical Society of Wisconsin.　　(58)

[164] Lewis, Meriwether, William Clark, *et al.*
[1804–1806] 1904–05. *Original Journals
of the Lewis and Clark Expedition, 1804–
1806; printed from the original manuscripts
. . . , including note-books, letters, maps,
etc., and the journals of Charles Floyd and
Joseph Whitehouse, now for the first time
published in full and exactly as written*, ed.
with intro., notes, and index by Reuben

Gold Thwaites. 8 vols. New York: Dodd, Mead & Company. Reprinted, New York: Antiquarian Press, 1959; New York: Arno, 1969.   (58)

[165] Liljeblad, Sven S. 1950. "Bannock 1: Phonemes." *International Journal of American Linguistics* 16:126–31.   (49)

*[166] ———. 1957. *Indian Peoples of Idaho.* Pocatello: Idaho State College.   (34)

[167] Linton, Ralph, ed. 1940. *Acculturation in Seven American Indian Tribes.* New York: D. Appleton-Century. Reprinted, Gloucester, Mass.: Peter Smith, 1963. See [86] [225].   (xi, 20)

[168] Loud, Llewellyn L., and M. R. Harrington. 1929. *Lovelock Cave.* University of California Publications in American Archaeology and Ethnology 25. Reprinted, New York: Kraus, 1965.   (6)

[169] Lowie, Robert H. 1909. "The Northern Shoshone." *American Museum of Natural History Anthropological Papers* 2:165–306. Reprinted, New York: AMS, 1975.   (29)

[170] ———. 1915. *Dances and Societies of the Plains Shoshone.* American Museum of

Natural History Anthropological Papers 11. (22)

[171] ———. 1919. "Sun Dance of the Shoshoni, Ute, and Hidatsa." *American Museum of Natural History Anthropological Papers* (16:387–411. (22, 33)

[172] ———. 1924. "Shoshonean Tales." *Journal of American Folk-Lore* 37:1–91. (19, 29)

[173] ———. 1924. *Notes on Shoshonean Ethnography.* American Museum of Natural History Anthropological Papers 20. (19, 29, 40)

[174] ———. 1939. "Ethnographic Notes on the Washo." *University of California Publications in Archaeology and Ethnology* 36:301–52. (45)

[175] ———. 1963. "Washo Texts." *Anthropological Linguistics* 5:1–30. (16, 45)

[176] Lyman, June, and Norma Denver. 1970. *Ute People: A Historical Study,* ed. Floyd O'Neil and John D. Sylvester. Salt Lake City: Uintah School District and the American West Center, University of Utah. (24)

[177]   McKern, W. C. 1978. *Western Colorado Petroglyphs*, ed. Douglas D. Scott. Denver: Colorado State Office, Bureau of Land Management.   (52)

[178]   McLane, Alvin R. 1975. *Pyramid Lake — A Bibliography*. Camp Nevada Monograph No. 1. Reno, Nevada.   (43)

*[179]   Madsen, Brigham D. 1958. *The Bannock of Idaho*. Caldwell, Idaho: The Caxton Printers.   (34, 65)

[180]   ———. 1967. "Shoshoni-Bannock Marauders on the Oregon Trail, 1859–1863." *Utah Historical Quarterly* 35:3–30.   (65)

*[181]   Mallery, Garrick. 1893. *Picture-writing of the American Indians*. Tenth Annual Report of the United States Bureau of Ethnology (1888–1889). Washington: Government Printing Office. Reprinted in 2 vols., New York: Dover, 1972.   (51)

*[182]   ———. 1886. *Pictographs of the North American Indians*. Fourth Annual Report of the United States Bureau of Ethnology. Washington: Government Printing Office.   (51)

[183] Malouf, Carling 1940. *The Gosiute Indians.* University of Utah Anthropological Papers No. 3. Reprinted, Salt Lake City: University of Utah Press, 1950. (33)

[184] ———. 1942. "Gosiute Peyotism" *American Anthropologist,* n. s. 44:93–103. (33)

[185] Malouf, Carling, and A. A. Malouf. 1945. "The Effects of Spanish Slavery on the Indians of the Intermountain West." *Southwestern Journal of Anthropology* 1:378–91. (26, 56)

*[186] Marquis, Arnold. 1974. *A Guide to America's Indians: Ceremonials, Reservations, and Museums.* Norman: University of Oklahoma Press. (69)

[187] Marsden W. L. 1923. "The Northern Paiute Language of Oregon." *University of California Publications in American Archaeology and Ethnology* 20:175–91. (48)

[188] Martineau, LaVan. 1973. *The Rocks Begin to Speak.* Las Vegas, Nevada: KC Publications. (54)

[189] Marwitt, J. P. 1973. *Median Village and Fremont Culture Regional Variations.* Uni-

versity of Utah Anthropological Papers
95.   (11)

[190] Merriam, A. P., and Warren L.
       d'Azevedo. 1957. "Washo Peyote
       Songs." *American Anthropologist*, n. s.
       59:615–41.   (46)

[191] Merriam, C. Hart. 1955. *Studies of
       California Indians*. Berkeley: University
       of California Press.   (38)

[192] Miller, Wick R. 1964. "The Shoshonean
       Languages of Uto-Aztecan: *University of
       California Publications in Linguistics*
       34:145–48.   (48)

[193] ———. 1966. "Anthropological Lin-
       guistics in the Great Basin," in *The Cur-
       rent Status of Anthropological Research in
       the Great Basin: 1964*, ed. W. L.
       d'Azevedo and others, pp. 75–112.
       Reno: Desert Research Institute of the
       University of Nevada. See [40].   (35, 49)

[194] ———. 1970. "Western Shoshoni
       Dialects," in *Language and Culture of
       Western North America: Essays in Honor of
       Sven S. Liljeblad*, ed. Earl H. Swanson,
       Jr., pp. 17–36. Pocatello: Idaho State
       University Press. See [312].   (49)

*[195]   ———. 1972. *Newe Natekwinappeh: Shoshoni Stories and Dictionary.* Salt Lake City: University of Utah Press.   (49)

[196]   ———. (in press). "The Numic Languages," in *Great Basin*, Vol. 11 of *Handbook of North American Indians.* See [11].   (50)

[197]   Monaghan, J. A. 1933. *The Bear Dance.* Denver: Colorado State Historical Society.   (21)

[198]   Mooney, James. 1896. *The Ghost Religion and the Sioux Outbreak of 1890.* In *Fourteenth Annual Report of the United States Bureau of Ethnology*, pp. 641–1136. Washington: Government Printing Office. Reprinted, Chicago: University of Chicago Press, 1965.   (36)

*[199]   Morgan, Dale Lowell. 1943. *The Humboldt, Highroad of the West.* New York: Farrar and Rinehart.   (62)

*[200]   ———. 1947. *The Great Salt Lake.* Indianapolis: Bobbs-Merrill Company.   (62)

[201]   ———. 1948. "The Administration of Indian Affairs in Utah, 1851–1858." *Pacific Historical Review* 17:383–409.   (62)

*[202]   ———. 1953. *Jedediah Smith and the Opening of the West.* Indianapolis: Bobbs-Merrill Company. Reprinted, Lincoln: University of Nebraska Press, 1964.   (61)

[203]   ———. 1953. "Miles Goodyear and the Founding of Ogden." *Utah Historical Quarterly* 21:195–218.   (61)

[204]   ———. 1954–1958. "Washakie and the Shoshoni: A Selection of Documents from the Records of the Utah Superintendency of Indian Affairs." *Annals of Wyoming* 25–30 (ten parts).   (34, 62)

[205]   ———. 1960. "The Ferries of the '49'ers." *Annals of Wyoming* 32:51–69, 169–203.   (62)

[206]   ———. 1968. "Utah before the Mormons." *Utah Historical Quarterly* 36:3–22.   (61)

[207]   Morgan, Dale L., and Carl I. Wheat. 1954. *Jedediah Smith and his Maps of the American West.* San Francisco: California Historical Society.   (62)

*[208] Morgan, Dale L., ed. 1941. *Utah: A Guide to the State.* New York: Hastings House. 2d ed., 1945.   (61)

[209] ———. 1959. *The Overland Diary of James A. Pritchard from Kentucky to California in 1849, with a Biography of Captain James A. Pritchard by Hugh Pritchard Williamson.* Denver: Fred Rosenstock.   (62)

[210] ———. 1963. *Overland in 1846; Diaries and Letters of the California and Oregon Trail.* 2 vols. Georgetown, California: Talisman Press.   (62)

[211] ———. [1822–1838] 1964. *The West of William H. Ashley; The International Struggle for the Fur Trade of the Missouri, the Rocky Mountains, and the Columbia, with Explorations beyond the Continental Divide, recorded in the Diaries and Letters of William H. Ashley and his Contemporaries, 1822–1838.* Denver: Old West Publishing Company.   (61)

[212] Morgan, Lewis Henry. 1878. "Journal of a Trip to Southwest Colorado and New Mexico," ed. Leslie A. White. *American Antiquity* 8:1–26.   (16)

*[213]   Murdock, George P., and Timothy J. O'Leary. 1975. *Ethnographic Bibliography of North America.* 5 vols. 4th edition. New Haven: Human Relations Area Files Press. See Vol. 3: *Far West and Pacific Coast.*   (viii, 35)

[214]   Murphy, Robert F., and Yolanda Murphy. 1960. "Shoshoni-Bannock Subsistence and Society." *University of California Anthropological Records* 16(7):293–338.   (33)

[215]   Natches, Gilbert. 1923. "Northern Paiute Verbs." *University of California Publications in American Archaeology and Ethnology* 20:245–59.   (48)

[216]   Nesbitt, P. E. 1968. *Stylistic Locales and Ethnographic Groups: Petroglyphs of the Lower Snake River.* Occasional Papers of the Idaho State Museum, Pocatello.   (53)

[217]   Nichols, Michael J. P. 1973. "Northern Paiute Historical Grammar." Ph.D. dissertation, University of California, Berkeley.   (49)

[218]   O'Connell, James F. 1975. *The Prehistory of Surprise Valley.* Ramona, Calif.: Ballena Press.   (42)

[219] Ogden, Peter Skene [1824–26] 1950. *Peter Skene Ogden's Snake Country Journals, 1824–25 and 1825–26*, ed. E. E. Rich and A. M. Johnson, with an introduction by W. Kaye Lamb. Publications of the Hudson's Bay Record Society 13. London: HBC. (58)

[220] ——— [1825]. 1952. "Peter Skene Ogden's Journal of His Expedition to Utah, 1825," ed. David E. Miller. *Utah Historical Quarterly* 20:160–86. (58)

[221] ———. [1826–27] 1961. *Peter Skene Ogden's Snake Country Journal, 1826–27*, ed. K. G. Davies and A. M. Johnson. Publications of the Hudson's Bay Record Society 23. London: HBC. (58)

[222] O'Neil, Floyd A. 1971. "The Reluctant Suzerainty: The Uintah and Ouray Reservation." *Utah Historical Quarterly* 39:129–44. (23, 66)

[223] Opler, Marvin K. 1939. "The Southern Ute Dog-Dance and its Reported Transmission to Taos." *New Mexican Anthropologist* 3:66–72. (20)

[224] ———. 1939. "The Ute Indian War of 1879." *El Palacio* 46 (November):225–62. (66)

[225] ———. 1940. "The Southern Ute of Colorado," in *Acculturation in Seven American Indian Tribes,* ed. Ralph Linton, pp. 119–206. See [167].   (20, 22)

[226] ———. 1940. "The Character and History of the Southern Ute Peyote Rite." *American Anthropologist,* n. s. 42:463–78.   (20)

[227] ———. 1941. "A Colorado Ute Bear Dance." *Southwestern Lore* 7:21–30.   (20, 21)

[228] ———. 1941. "The Integration of the Sun Dance in Ute Religion." *American Anthropologist,* n. s. 43:550–72.   (20, 22)

[229] ———. 1942. "Fact and Fancy in Ute Peyotism." *American Anthropologist,* n. s. 44:151–59.   (20)

[230] ———. 1943. "The Origins of Comanche and Ute." *American Anthropologist,* n. s. 45:155–58.   (20)

[231] Owen, Roger C. 1965. "The Patrilocal Band: A Linguistically and Culturally Hybrid Social Unit." *American Anthropologist,* n. s. 67:675–90.   (30)

[232] Park, Willard Z. 1938. *Shamanism in Western North America.* Northwestern

University Studies in Social Sciences No. 2. (37)

*[233] Patterson, Edna B., Louise A. Ulph, and Victor Goodwin. 1969. *Nevada's Northeastern Frontier.* Sparks, Nevada: Western Printing and Publishing Company. (35)

*[234] Patterson, Edna B. 1972. *Sagebrush Doctors.* Springville, Utah: Art City Publishing Company. (34)

*[235] Powell, John Wesley. 1875. *Exploration of the Colorado River of the West and its Tributaries, Explored in 1869, 1870, 1871, and 1872 under the Direction of the Secretary of the Smithsonian Institution.* Washington: Government Printing Office. Reprinted, in abridged ed., with intro. by Wallace Stegner, Chicago: University of Chicago Press, 1957. New ed., New York: Dover, 1961. (64)

[236] ———. 1826–1880. [manuscripts on the Numic Peoples of Western North America]. See Fowler and Fowler [60]. (16, 35, 36)

[237] Powers, Stephen. [1875] 1970. "Stephen Powers' 'The Life and Culture of the Washo and Paiutes'," ed.

Don D. Fowler and Catherine S. Fowler. *Ethnohistory* 17:117–49. See [59]. (38)

[238]   ———. 1877. *Tribes of California*. U.S. Geographical and Geological Survey of the Rocky Mountain Region *Contributions to North American Ethnology* 3. Washington: Government Printing Office for the Department of the Interior. Reprinted, Berkeley: University of California Press, 1976. (38, 45)

[239]   Price, John A. 1962. "Washo Economy." Master's thesis, University of Utah. (46)

[240]   ———. 1980. *The Washo Indians: History, Life Cycle, Religion, Technology, Economy and Modern Life.* Nevada State Museum Occasional Papers 4. Carson City, Nevada. (46)

[241]   Reagan, Albert B. 1930. "The Bear Dance of the Ouray Ute." *Wisconsin Archaeologist* 9:148–50. (21)

[242]   ———. 1931. "The Pictographs of Ashley and Dry Fork Valleys in Northeastern Utah." *Transactions of the Kansas Academy of Science* 34:168–216. (53)

[243] Reed, Erik K. 1966. *Utah Crania of the Historic Period and Basin Shoshonean Physical Type.* University of Utah Anthropological Papers 83.   (67)

[244] Reed, Verner Z. 1893. "The Southern Ute Indians." *The Californian* 4:488–505.   (19)

[245] ———. 1894. "Three Indian Chiefs: Savaro, Ignacio and Buckskin Charley." *The Great Divide* 11(2):37–40.   (19)

[246] ———. 1896. "The Ute Bear Dance." *American Anthropologist,* n. s. 9:237–44. (19, 21)

[247] Riddell, F. A. 1960. *The Archaeology of the Karlo Site (Las-7), California.* University of California Archaeological Survey Reports 53:1–110.   (7)

[248] Roberts, Bertram L. 1965. "Descendants of the *Numu.*" *The Masterkey* 39(1–2):13–22, 66–76.   (42)

*[249] Rogers, Malcolm. J. 1966. "The Ancient Hunters—Who Were They?" In *Ancient Hunters of the Far West,* ed. Richard F. Pourade, pp. 23–110. San

Diego: The Union-Tribune Publishing
Company.   (5)

[250] Ross, Alexander. 1855. *The Fur Hunters
of the Far West; A Narrative of Adventures
in the Oregon and Rocky Mountains.* . . .
London: Smith, Elder and Company.
Reprinted, Norman: University of Oklahoma Press, 1956.   (28, 33, 47, 59)

[251] Rudy, J. R., and R. D. Stirland. 1950.
*An Archeological Reconnaissance in Wash-
ington County, Utah.* University of Utah
Anthropological Papers 9.   (11)

*[252] Russell, Osborne. 1914. *Journal of a
Trapper; or, Nine Years in the Rocky Moun-
tains: 1834–1843.* . . . Boise, Idaho:
Syms-York Company. New ed., Aubrey
L. Haines, ed., Portland: Oregon His-
torical Society, 1955.   (28, 59)

[253] Sapir, Edward. 1930–1931. *Southern
Paiute, A Shoshonean Language.* Proceedings of the American Academy of Arts
and Science 65.   (25, 48)

[254] Schaafsma, Polly. 1970. *Survey Report of
the Rock Art of Utah.* Salt Lake City: Division of State History.   (53)

[255] ———. 1971. *The Rock Art of Utah: A Study from the Donald Scott Collection, Peabody Museum, Harvard University.* Peabody Museum of Archaeology and Ethnology Paper 65. Cambridge, Mass.   (53)

[256] Schoolcraft, Henry Rowe. 1851–57. *Historical and Statistical Information Respecting the History, Conditions and Prospects of the Indian Tribes of the United States.* 6 vols. Philadelphia: Lippincott, Grambo. Index comp. by Francis S. Nichols. Washington: Government Printing Office, 1954. Reprinted in 7 vols., including index. New York: AMS, 1969.   (16, 28, 51)

[257] Service, Elman R. 1962. *Primitive Social Organization: An Evolutionary Perspective.* New York: Random House. Reprinted, 1971.   (30)

[258] Shimkin, Demitri B. 1939. "Some Interactions of Culture, Needs, and Personalities among the Wind River Shoshone." Ph.D. dissertation, University of California, Berkeley.   (32)

[259] ———. 1947. "Childhood and Development among the Wind River Sho-

shone." *University of California Anthropological Records* 5(5):289–325.   (32)

[260]   ———. 1947. "Wind River Shoshone Ethnogeography." *University of California Anthropological Records* 5(4):245–288.   (32)

[261]   ———. 1953. "The Wind River Shoshone Sun Dance." *Bureau of American Ethnology Bulletin* 151:397–484. Washington: Government Printing Office.   (32)

[262]   Shimkin, Demitri B., and Russell M. Reid. 1970. "Socio-Cultural Persistence among Shoshoneans of the Carson River Basin (Nevada)," in *Language and Cultures of Western North America,* ed. Earl H. Swanson, Jr. pp. 172–200. See [312].   (42)

[263]   Shutler, Richard, Jr. 1961. *Lost City: Pueblo Grande de Nevada.* Nevada State Museum Anthropological Papers 5. Carson City.   (3, 9)

[264]   ———. 1967. "Archaeology of Tule Springs" and "Cultural Chronology in Southern Nevada," in *Pleistocene Studies in Southern Nevada,* eds. H. H. Worm-

ington and D. Ellis, pp. 298–308.
Nevada State Museum Anthropological
Papers No. 13. Carson City. See [359].   (3)

[265] Siskin, Edgar E. 1968. "The Impact of
the Peyote Cult upon Shamanism
among the Washo Indians." Ph.D. dissertation, Yale University. Ann Arbor:
University Microfilms.   (46)

[266] Smith, Anne M. 1937. "The Material
Culture of the Northern Ute." Master's
thesis, Yale University.   (20)

[267] ———. 1939. "An Analysis of Basin
Mythology." Ph.D. dissertation, Yale
University.   (20)

[268] ———. 1974. *Ethnography of the Northern Utes.* Museum of New Mexico Papers in Anthropology 17. Santa Fe.   (20, 22)

[269] Smith, Elmer R. 1952. *The Archaeology
of Deadman Cave, Utah: A Revision.* University of Utah Anthropological Papers
10.   (11)

*[270] Sprague, Marshall. 1957. *Massacre: The
Tragedy of White River.* Boston: Little
Brown and Company. Reprinted, Lin-

coln: University of Nebraska Press, 1980.   (66)

[271] Spuhler, James N. 1954. "Some Problems in the Physical Anthropology of the American Southwest." *American Anthropologist,* n. s. 56:604–25.   (67)

[272] Stegner, Wallace. 1954. *Beyond the Hundredth Meridian: John Wesley Powell and the Second Opening of the West.* Boston: Houghton, Mifflin Company. Reprinted, 1962.   (64)

[273] Stenberg, Molly P. 1946. "The Peyote Cult among Wyoming Indians." *University of Wyoming Publications* 12(4):85–156. Laramie.   (33)

[274] Stevens, David Walter. 1965. "Capital as a Determinant of Economic Growth: Allocation in a Tri-Ethnic Community." Ph.D. dissertation, University of Colorado.   (25)

[275] Steward, Julian H. 1929. "Petroglyphs of California and Adjoining States." *University of California Publications in Archaeology and Ethnology* 24(2):47–238.   (52, 53)

[276] ———. 1932. "A Uintah Ute Bear Dance, March, 1931." *American Anthropologist,* n. s. 34:263–73. (21)

[277] ———. 1933. *Early Inhabitants of Western Utah. Part 1 —Mounds and House Types.* University of Utah Bulletin 23. Salt Lake City. (10)

[278] ———. 1933. *Ethnography of the Owens Valley Paiute.* Berkeley: University of California Press. Reprinted, New York: Kraus, 1965. (40)

[279] ———. 1933. *Archaeological Problems of the Northern Periphery of the Southwest.* Museum of Northern Arizona Bulletin 5. Flagstaff. (10)

[280] ———. 1936. *Pueblo Material Culture in Western Utah.* University of New Mexico Bulletin 287. Albuquerque. (10)

[281] ———. 1937. *Ancient Caves of the Great Salt Lake Region.* Bureau of American Ethnology Bulletin 116. Washington: Government Printing Office. (10)

[282] ———. 1938. *Basin-Plateau Aboriginal Sociopolitical Groups.* Bureau of Ameri-

can Ethnology Bulletin 120. Washington: Government Printing Office. Reprinted, Salt Lake City: University of Utah Press, 1970.   (29)

[283]   ———. 1939. *Notes on Hillers' photographs of the Paiute and Ute Indians taken on the Powell Expedition of 1873.* Smithsonian Miscellaneous Collections 98(18).   (26)

[284]   ———. 1941. "Archaeological Reconnaissance of Southern Utah." *Bureau of American Ethnology Bulletin* 128:277–356. Washington: Government Printing Office.   (10)

[285]   ———. 1941. *Culture Element Distribution: XIII. Nevada Shoshone.* University of California Anthropological Records 4(2).   (29, 41)

[286]   ———. 1943. *Culture Element Distribution: XXIII. Northern and Gosiute Shoshoni.* University of California Anthropological Records 8(3).   (29)

[287]   ———. 1955. *Theory of Culture Change: The Methodology of Multilinear Evolution.* Urbana: University of Illinois Press. Reprinted, 1976.   (29)

[288] ———. 1970. "The Foundation of Basin-Plateau Shoshonean Society," in *Languages and Cultures of Western North America*, ed. Earl H. Swanson, Jr., pp. 113–51. See [312]. (42)

[289] Steward, Julian H., and Erminie Wheeler-Voegelin. 1974. *The Northern Paiute Indians*. United States Indian Claims Commission, American Indian Ethnohistory Series, *Paiute Indians* 3. New York: Garland. (41)

[290] Stewart, Omer C. 1939. "The Northern Paiute Bands." *University of California Anthropological Records* 2:127–49. (41, 42)

[291] ———. 1941. "Culture Element Distributions XIV: Northern Paiute." *University of California Anthropological Records* 4:361–446. (38, 41, 44)

[292] ———. 1941. "The Southern Ute Peyote Cult." *American Anthropologist*, n. s. 43:303–08. (21)

[293] ———. 1942. "Culture Element Distributions XVIII: Ute—Southern Paiute." *University of California Anthropological Records* 6:231–355. (20, 22, 26)

[294]   ———. 1944. "Washo-Northern Paiute Peyotism, A Study in Acculturation." *University of California Publications in Archaeology and Ethnology* 40:63–136.   (37, 45)

[295]   ———. 1948. *Ute Peyotism: A Study of a Cultural Complex.* University of Colorado Series in Anthropology No. 1.   (21)

[296]   ———. 1952. "Southern Ute Adjustment to Modern Living," in *Acculturation in the Americas*, ed. Sol Tax, pp. 80–87. Proceedings of the Twenty-ninth International Congress of Americanists. Chicago: University of Chicago Press.   (24)

[297]   ———. 1956. "Three Gods for Joe." *Tomorrow* 4:71–76.   (37)

[298]   ———. 1965. "The Shoshone of the Great Basin," in *The Native Americans: Prehistory and Ethnology of North American Indians*, ed. Robert F. Spencer and Jesse D. Jennings. New York: Harper and Row.   (34)

[299]   ———. 1965. "The Shoshoni: Their History and Social Organization." *Idaho Yesterdays* 9(3):2–5,28.   (34)

[300] ———. 1966. "Tribal Distribution and Boundaries in the Great Basin." In *The Current Status of Anthropological Research in the Great Basin: 1964*, pp. 167–238. Reno: Desert Research Institute, University of Nevada. (30)

[301] ———. 1966. "Ute Indians: Before and After White Contact." *Utah Historical Quarterly* 34:38–61. (23)

[302] ———. 1970. "The Question of Bannock Territory." In *Languages and Cultures of Western North America*, ed. Earl H. Swanson, Jr., pp. 201–31. See [312]. (33)

[303] ———. 1971. *Ethnohistorical Bibliography of the Ute Indians of Colorado*. University of Colorado Studies, Series in Anthropology No. 18. (25)

[304] ———. 1977. "Contemporary Document on Wovoka (Jack Wilson) Prophet of the Ghost Dance of 1890." *Ethnohistory* 24(3):219–22. (37)

[305] ———. 1978. "The Western Shoshone of Nevada and the U.S. Government, 1863–1950," in *Selected Papers from the Fourteenth Great Basin Anthropological*

Conference, ed. Donald R. Tuohy, pp. 77–114. Socorro, New Mexico: Ballena Press.   (65)

[306] ———. 1980. "Temoke Band of Shoshone and the Oasis Concept." *Nevada Historical Society Quarterly* 23(4):246–61.   (21, 30, 65)

[307] Stoffle, Richard W., and Michael J. Evans. 1979. *Kaibab Paiute History: The Early Years*. Kaibab Paiute Tribe Cultural Heritage Pamphlet 1. Fredonia, Arizona: Kaibab Paiute Tribe.   (26)

[308] Swadesh, Frances L. 1966. "Hispanic Americans of the Ute Frontier, 1694–1960." Ph.D. dissertation, University of Colorado.   (25)

[309] ———. 1974. *Los Primeros Pobladores: Hispanic Americans of the Ute Frontier*. South Bend: University of Notre Dame Press.   (25, 56)

[310] Swadesh, Morris. 1954. "Time Depths of American Linguistic Groups." *American Anthropologist*, n. s. 56:361–64.   (48)

[311] Swanson, Earl H., Jr., ed. 1968. *Utaztekan Prehistory*. Occasional Papers of the

Idaho State University Museum No. 22. Pocatello. (50)

[312] ———, ed. 1970. *Languages and Cultures of Western North America: Essays in Honor of Sven S. Liljeblad.* Pocatello: The Idaho State University Press. See [92] [194] [262] [288] [302]. (xii)

[313] Thomas, D. H., and T. C. Thomas. 1972. "New Data on Rock Art Chronology in the Central Great Basin." *Tebiwa* 15(1):64–71. (53)

[314] Thomas, David Hurst. 1973. "An Empirical Test for Steward's Model of Great Basin Settlement Patterns." *American Antiquity* 38:155–76. (30)

[315] Thompson, David. 1916. *David Thompson's Narrative of his Explorations in Western America, 1784–1812*, ed. J. B. Tyrell. Toronto: The Champlain Society. New ed., ed. with intro. and notes by Richard Glover, 1962. Also printed as *David Thompson and the Lewis and Clark Expedition*, intro. by Peter Grossman, Vancouver: British Columbia Library's Press, 1959. (57)

[316] Thompson, Gregory C. 1971. "Southern Ute Lands, 1848–1899: The Creation of a Reservation." Master's Thesis, University of Utah.   (65)

[317] Trenholm, Virginia Cole, and Maurine Carley. 1964. *The Shoshonis: Sentinels of the Rockies.* Norman: University of Oklahoma Press. Reprinted, 1976.   (34)

[318] Thwaites, Reuben Gold, ed. 1904–1907. *Early Western Travels, 1748–1846: A Series of Annotated Reprints of some of the best and rarest contemporary volumes of travel, descriptive of the Aborigines and Social and Economic Conditions in the Middle and Far West, during the Period of Early American Settlement.* 32 vols. Cleveland: The Arthur H. Clark Company. See vols 31–32 for index. Reprinted, New York: AMS, 1966.   (28)

[319] ———, ed. 1905. *Original Journals of the Lewis and Clark Expedition, 1804–1806.* 8 vols. New York: Dodd, Mead and Company. Reprinted, New York: Antiquarian Press, 1959; New York: Arno, 1969.   (28)

[320] Tuohy, Donald R. 1969. *Breakage, Burin Facets, and the Probable Technological*

*Linkage among Lake Mohave, Silver Lake,
and other Varieties of Paleo-Indian Projectile Points in the Desert West.* Nevada
State Museum Anthropological Papers
No. 14. Carson City.   (5)

[321] ———, ed. 1978. *Selected Papers from the
14th Great Basin Anthropological Conference (1974).* Socorro, New Mexico: Ballena Press.   (70)

[322] Tyler, S. Lyman, 1951. "Before Escalante; an Early History of the Yuta
Indians and the Area North of New
Mexico." Ph.D. dissertation, University
of Utah.   (18, 56)

[323] ———. 1951. "The Yuta Indians before
1680." *Western Humanities Review* 5
(Spring):153–63.   (56)

[324] ———. 1954. "The Spaniard and the
Ute." *Utah Historical Quarterly* 22:343–
61.   (56)

[325] ———. 1964. *The Ute People: A Bibliographical Checklist.* Provo, Utah:
Brigham Young University Press.   (18)

[326] Tyzzer, Robert Neal III. 1974. "An Investigation of the Demographic and

Genetic Structure of a Southwestern American Indian Population: The Southern Ute Tribe of Colorado." Ph.D. dissertation, University of Colorado. Ann Arbor: University Microfilms. (25)

[327] Underhill, Ruth M. 1941. *The Northern Paiute Indians of California and Nevada*. Lawrence, Kansas: Bureau of Indian Affairs Publications Service, Haskell Institute. Reprinted, New York: AMS, 1980. (40)

*[328] Uintah-Ouray Ute Tribe. 1977. *A Brief History of the Ute People*. Fort Duchesne, Utah: Unitah-Ouray Ute Tribe. (23)

*[329] ———. 1977. *The Ute People*. Fort Duchesne, Utah: Uintah-Ouray Ute Tribe. (23)

*[330] ———. 1977. *Ute Ways*. Fort Duchesne, Utah: Uintah-Ouray Tribe. (28)

*[331] ———. 1977. *The Way It Was Told*. Fort Duchesne, Utah: Uintah-Ouray Ute Tribe. (23)

*[332] ———. 1977. *The Ute System of Government*. Fort Duchesne, Utah: Uintah-Ouray Ute Tribe. (23)

[333] United States Congress. House of Representatives. 1953. *Report with respect to the House resolution authorizing the Committee on Interior and Insular Affairs to conduct an Investigation of the Bureau of Indian Affairs.* Pursuant to H. Res. 698 (82nd Cong.). Union Calendar No. 790, House Report No. 2503, 82d Cong., 2d sess. (68)

[334] United States Department of Commerce. 1974. *Federal and State Indian Reservations and Indian Trust Areas.* Washington: Government Printing Office. (69)

[335] United States Indian Claims Commission. 1959. *Findings of Fact.* The Washoe Tribe of the States of Nevada and California vs. the United States. Docket No. 288. (7 Ind. Cl. Com. 266), March 20, 1959. Available on microfiche, New York: Clearwater. (45)

[336] ———. 1974. "Commission Findings on the Paiute Indians." In David Agee Horr, ed., American Indian Ethnohistory Series, California and Basin-Plateau Indians, *Paiute Indians* 5. New York: Garland. (65)

[337] Voget, Fred W. 1948. "The Diffusion of
       the Wind River Shoshone Sundance to
       the Crow Indians of Montana." Ph.D.
       dissertation, Yale University.   (33)

[338] ———. 1948. "Individual Motivation in
       the Diffusion of the Wind River
       Shoshone Sundance to the Crow In-
       dians." *American Anthropologist*, n. s.
       50:634–46.   (33)

[339] ———. 1950. "A Shoshone Innovator."
       American Anthropologist, n. s. 52:53–63. (33)

[340] ———. 1953. "Current Trends in the
       Wind River Shoshone Sun Dance."
       Bureau of American Ethnology Bulletin
       151:485–99. Washington: Government
       Printing Office.   (33)

[341] von Werlhof, Jay C. 1965. *Rock Art of
       Owens Valley, California*. University of
       California Archaeological Survey Re-
       ports 65.   (52)

*[342] Walker River Paiute Tribe. 1975. *Walker
        River Paiutes: A Tribal History*. Schurz,
        Nevada: Walker River Paiute Tribe.   (66)

*[343] Walker, Deward E., Jr. 1978. *Indians of
        Idaho*. Boise: University Press of Idaho. (35)

[344] Watson, Chandler B. 1967. "Recollections of the Bannock War." *Oregon Historical Quarterly* 68:317–29.   (65)

[345] Wedel, Waldo R. 1954. "Earthenware and Steatite Vessels from Northwestern Wyoming." *American Antiquity* 19:403–09.   (14)

[346] Wheat, Carl I. 1957–1963. *Mapping the Transmississippi West, 1540–1861.* 5 vols. San Francisco: The Institute of Historical Cartography. Also see [207].   (62, 66)

[347] Wheat, Joe Ben. 1972. *The Olsen-Chubbuck Site: A Paleo-Indian Bison Kill.* Society for American Archaeology, *Memoir* No. 26. Washington, D.C.: Society for American Archaeology. Also issued as *American Antiquity* 37(1).   (1)

[348] Wheat, Margaret M. 1967. *Survival Arts of the Primitive Paiutes.* Reno: University of Nevada Press.   (42)

[349] Wheeler-Voegelin, Erminie. 1955–1956. "The Northern Paiute of Central Oregon: A Chapter in Treaty-Making." *Ethnohistory* 2:95–132, 146–82, 241–72; 3:1–10.   (41)

[350] Whiting, Beatrice Blyth. 1950. *Paiute Sorcery*. Viking Fund Publications in Anthropology No. 15. New York. Reprinted, New York: Johnson, 1971. (40, 41)

[351] Wilke, Philip J., ed. 1979. *Journal of California and Great Basin Anthropology* 1(1). Banning, California: Malki Museum, Inc., Morengo Indian Reservation. (69)

[352] Wilmsen, Edwin N. 1974. *Lindenmeier: A Pleistocene Hunting Society*. New York: Harper and Row. (2)

[353] Wilmsen, Edwin N. and Frank H. H. Roberts, Jr. 1975. *Lindenmeier: Concluding Report of Investigations 1934–1974*. Smithsonian Contributions to Anthropology 24. (2)

*[354] Wilson, E. N. 1919. *The White Indian Boy. The Story of Uncle Nick among the Shoshones*, revised ed., ed. Howard R. Driggs. Yonkers-on-the-Hudson, New York: World Book Company. (34)

[355] Witherspoon, Younger T. 1961. "Cultural Influences on Ute Learning." Ph.D. dissertation, University of Utah. (23)

[356] Work, John. 1912–1913. "Journal of John Work, Covering Snake Country Expedition of 1830–31," ed. T. C. Elliot. *Oregon Historical Quarterly* 13:363–71; 14:280–314. (59)

[357] ———. 1923. *The Journal of John Work, a Chief-Trader of the Hudson's Bay Company, during his Expedition from Vancouver to the Flatheads and Blackfeet of the Pacific Northwest, edited and with an account of the Fur Trade in the Northwest, and life of Work, by William S. Lewis and Paul C. Phillips.* Cleveland: The Arthur H. Clark Company. (59)

[358] ———. 1945. *Fur Brigade to the Bonaventura. John Work's California Expedition 1832–1833 for the Hudson's Bay Company*, ed. Alice Bay Maloney with foreword by Herbert E. Bolton. San Francisco: California Historical Society. (59)

*[359] Wormington, Hannah Marie. [1939] 1970. *Ancient Man in North America.* 7th ed., revised. Denver: The Denver Museum of Natural History. (1, 2)

[360] Wormington, Hannah Marie, and D. Ellis, eds. 1967. *Pleistocene Studies in*

Southern Nevada. Nevada State Museum Anthropological Papers No. 13. Carson City.   (5)

[361] Wyeth, Nathaniel Jarvis. 1853. "Indian Tribes of the South Pass of the Rocky Mountains, The Salt Lake Basin . . .", in *Historical and Statistical Information Respecting the History, Conditions and Prospects of the Indian Tribes of the United States*, collected and prepared by Henry Rowe Schoolcraft. Part 1: 204–28. See [256].   (47, 59)

[362] Young, Karl E. 1933. "Bear Dance." *Improvement Era* 36(6):328–31.   (21)

[363] ————. 1972. "Sun Dance at Whiterocks, 1919." *Utah Historical Quarterly* 40:233–41.   (22)

[364] Zigmond, Maurice L. 1979. "Gotlieb Adam Steiner and the G. A. Steiner Museum." *Journal of California and Great Basin Anthropology* 1(2):322–30.   (46)

The Newberry Library
Center for the History of the American Indian
Founding Director: D'Arcy McNickle
Director: Francis Jennings

Established in 1972 by the Newberry Library, in conjunction with the Committee on Institutional Cooperation of eleven midwestern universities, the Center makes the resources of one of America's foremost research libraries in the Humanities available to those interested in improving the quality and effectiveness of teaching American Indian history. The Newberry's collections include some 110,000 volumes on the history of the American Indian and offer specialized resources for studying historical aspects of Indian-White relations and Indian linguistics. The Center also assists Native Americans engaged in writing tribal histories and developing educational materials.

ADVISORY COMMITTEE

Chairman: Alfonso Ortiz
University of New Mexico